Travelman

Liberty & Livelihood

A PORTRAIT OF LIFE IN RURAL BRITAIN

EDITORS
JOANNA EEDE
WILLIAM MOLLETT

in association with
the Countryside Alliance

FOR THOMAS

ACKNOWLEDGEMENTS

Catherine Born, Andrew Bruce, Louise Cavanagh
John Eede, Judith Eede, Kashish Gupta, Henny Goddard
Nigel Henson, Cleo Johnson, Rose Murray, Sarah Mollett
Harry Ram, Janene Spencer, Alexander Waugh

This book is celebration of the countryside as seen through the eyes of many of today's leading exponents and enthusiasts. Their contributions are accompanied by a wide array of arresting and unusual photographs selected from a photographic competition sponsored by Travelman Publishing and launched by *The Daily Telegraph* and the Countryside Alliance.

We are indebted to all the contributors who have generously submitted articles for inclusion in the book and to the photographers for sending in so many original negatives and transparencies, in the knowledge that a royalty from this book would be donated to the Countryside Alliance.

First published in 2003 by
Travelman Publishing
18 King Edward Buildings
629 Fulham Road
London
SW6 5UH
www.travelman.co.uk

A catalogue record for this book is available from the British Library
ISBN 1-86092-024-1

Printed in Scotland by
Scotprint

Contents

THATCHERS, SOMERSET
© W. P. Andrews

Nelson
Antony Beevor

When I was a small boy in east Kent in the 1950s, my hero was a woodsman called Nelson. Today, of course, he would be called a tree surgeon. He had white hair, a smiling, cherubic face and clear blue eyes. He was one of the kindest people I had ever met, as well as one of the bravest, working high in the branches of tall trees. In those days, there were no hydraulic towers and nobody wore hard hats.

My mother was the same age as Nelson and remembered him from her childhood. Nelson, the only son of a young widow, had been sent to the village school dressed as a girl. My mother told me this detail years later after she had heard a programme on the wireless. Apparently, in certain parts of the countryside, a belief had persisted up to the First World War that fairies would snatch a solitary male child. As a result, fearful mothers tried to pass their sons off as girls until the time they reached puberty. I immediately wondered whether my childhood hero had been teased or bullied at school. He certainly would have been hounded today in any urban playground. But in the real countryside community, one still finds a spontaneous kindness and tolerance of eccentricities unimaginable in city life. Today, fortunately, nobody would be frightened by superstition into sending a boy to school dressed as a girl, yet peculiarities still tend to be cherished. Even difficult characters are spoken of with a grudging admiration, if only because they provide endless food for conversation.

The pace of change – technological, economic and above all social – has been bewildering for everyone, yet up to now, the family and community has suffered far less disintegration in the countryside than in the city. But now the economic basis of farming and the traditional rural economy are in mortal danger. The attitude in Whitehall seems to be, 'Well, in the 1980s it was coal mining and the old heavy

industries which died, now it's farming'. Politicians and bureaucrats then go on to talk of preserving the landscape with barely a mention of those who have always worked and lived there. It is discussed as if it were nothing more than a 'leisure resource' for jaded city-dwellers to escape to. Perhaps that fate is already inescapable. But how on earth can you preserve any sort of real countryside – as opposed to a few Disney-fied national park nature trails – without the knowledge, the skills and the character of those very people whose families have maintained it for generations?

The historian Antony Beevor was brought up in Kent, and educated at Winchester and Sandhurst. He has published four novels and six works of non-fiction, including *Stalingrad*, which won the first Samuel Johnson Prize and the Wolfson Prize, and *Berlin, the Downfall*.

THATCHING (OPPOSITE) © W.P. Andrews

The use of straw or grasses as a building material for roofing dates back to the Bronze Age and was the most common form of roof-covering in Britain until the end of medieval times. It was still the most practical solution until the mid-19th century when the introduction of the railways meant that cheap slate from Wales was easily available. Wheat straw was the most widely used until the introduction of the combine harvester in 1950s which produced shorter wheat. Alternative materials such as broom, sedge, sallow, and flax grass were used instead, but East Anglia reed is now the most common. Distinct regional differences exist, and individual thatchers will have their own style, with the treatment of ridges, eaves and gables varying around the country.

Thatcher in Devizes
© Deborah Husk

The Field Hedge
Robin Page

Why do I always draw the short straw? The short straw being, in this instance, writing an article about hedge-laying. As far as I'm concerned, there are two totally inadequate words in the English language: the first being 'hedge'. Hedges come in all shapes and sizes: high hedges, low hedges, fat hedges, thin hedges, tidy hedges, unkempt hedges, old hedges and young hedges.

The second inadequate word is 'green'. There is a different shade of green for every different type of hedge – in fact there are so many shades of green that a single word does not do justice to the extraordinary variety of tinctures and textures – light green, dark green, metallic green, olive green, not to mention spring greens, lush greens and gorgeous dripping greens.

The hedge has a host of uses – not least to keep things in and to keep things out. They act as ornaments, boundaries, mazes, follies and integral parts of 'landscape architecture'. Sometimes there is no great difference between a boundary hedge and a length of green 'landscape architecture' – except in price.

The hedge that I like is the field hedge. The field hedge turned peasant Britain into farmed Britain. During the 'enclosures', the field hedge combined with the ancient hedges that marked parish and estate boundaries. In my part of Britain they were predominantly hawthorn, but in other areas with other soils and other traditions there were, and are, beech, holly and even yew hedges.

The older the hedge, the greater the variety of trees and shrubs that can be found within it. Different seeds arrive courtesy of birds and animals. Oak, elm, ash, spindle, field maple, crab apple, elder, privet, wild rose, guelder rose, blackthorn, blackberry, buckthorn, dogwood and many others turn hedges into varied, living entities. A multitude of birds, animals and insects make their homes within hedges. The woodland hedge is thus the richest part of a wood for wildlife. A hedge, in effect, provides miles of woodland edge.

We have never pulled out one hedge on our small farm. From a practical perspective, they help to keep the cattle in. From a more sensory perspective they give us great pleasure. We love finding ribbons of scented 'may',

NELSON RUSSELL, HEDGE-LAYER
© Sally Mackenzie
Aged 89 and still competing in hedge-laying competitions,
Nelson Russell has worked on the land since he was 11 years old.

Dry Stone Walling
© John Randle

hearing the call of the mistle-thrush, the green woodpecker and the all-too-rare cuckoo. We love discovering the rich hedgerow harvest of berries, fruit and butterflies. Some of our hedges are wild and struggling, creating warm fields, sheltered from the wind with their own microclimates. I feel sorry for those people who have ripped out their hedges or who, obsessed with tidiness, trim them before the fieldfares and redwings have taken the berries.

Winter was when my late father, Charlie, would lay the hedges with Jim on a rotation of seven or eight years. They were days of great laughter, skill and woodsmoke. Now, my old hedge-laying friend Badger Walker arrives and we 'play' at hedge-laying. Badger wins prizes and loves his hedges – in fact his love has grown so great that he has abandoned his 'real' job as a computer expert to become a professional hedge-layer. We both regard it as a considerable step up the social ladder.

Short straw? I've changed my mind. I didn't draw the short straw to write about hedges; it has been a privilege. Long may the hedge be part of the traditional English farming landscape – a landscape that should put people back in touch with nature, farming and beauty.

Robin Page writes the fortnightly 'Country Diary' in *The Daily Telegraph* and has written for the *Spectator*. He is author of *The Decline of an English Village; The Fox and the Orchid; The Wildlife of the Royal Estates; A Peasant's Diary; Gone to the Dogs* and *Vocal Yokel*. He presented the BBC's *One Man and His Dog* and in 1993 founded the Countryside Restoration Trust. He stood for the Referendum Party in the 1997 General Election.

DRY STONE WALLING (OPPOSITE)

Dry stone walls have been a feature of the British landscape for hundreds of years especially in upland farming areas where they replace hedges and fences as field boundaries. Known as dry stone walling from the technique of building without mortar to bind the stones, they typically consist of an outer layer of large stones concealing a core of smaller stones or earth.

Dry stone walls are built in the local available stone, such as limestone in the Cotswolds or slate in Cornwall, and there are also different regional styles, due in part to working in these different materials.

This ancient craft is now returning to many parts for economic as well as environmental reasons. Built well, they can last for hundreds of years with little maintenance, and their strong visual appeal is also increasingly popular with landscape gardeners.

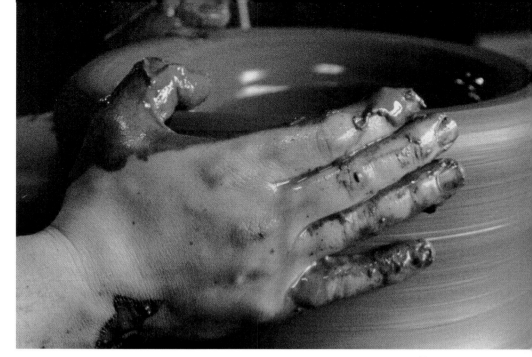

POTTER
© Ken Wheller

CABINETMAKER
© Andrew Gilpin

SMOKY FARRIER
© W. P. Andrews

A Living Countryside
Jeanette Winterson

BENDING HORSE SHOES
© Samantha Lewis

The typical English village, with its pub, church, shops and crafts, is more of a fantasy than a reality, but it is a fantasy we are reluctant to give up, perhaps because few of us are as well adapted to modern life as we would like to believe.

The modern world is a twenty-four hour emergency zone, where human beings are pressed for time and space, working longer hours, sometimes for more money, but with very little sign of content. When we are not working, we are shopping, and when we are not shopping, we are jumping in the car trying to entertain ourselves. One of the saddest summer sights is the clogged motorways jammed with people 'having fun'.

The decline of vigorous village life is a complex layer of cause and effect with a long history. We could reverse that decline, but that would take radical changes at every level. Within our gift, right now, is the chance to prevent further decline. By supporting rural jobs, whether craft, profession or labour, we allow people to stay on the land and connected to it. This is vital for the maintenance of our countryside, and something else, just as precious: we need a living countryside for the sake of our souls.

The farmer, the farrier, the dry stone waller, the reed-gatherer, the thatcher, the gamekeeper – make your own list – do the invisible work of the countryside, and allow us to enjoy what we think of as quintessential England. Often these people are not well paid, and don't own their own houses; what they stand for is a way of life where money is not everything, and where other values are still held to be important.

FARRIERS

Farriers, or shoesmiths, have been used in agriculture for centuries and there is evidence that iron shoes were used for horses before the Roman invasion. The widespread use of horses in agriculture led to the development of this skill and records show that the farriers of the City of London formed a fellowship in 1356. Today it is an offence for an unregistered person to describe himself as a farrier or shoesmith, or to carry out the work of farriery. There are 2,800 qualified farriers working throughout Britain, with rigorous training and exams to ensure that horses are properly shod. With the popularity of horse racing and other equestrian sports there is great demand for their services; there are seven farriers serving with the King's Troop of the Royal Horse Artillery, preparing the horses for ceremonial occasions.

I live in the countryside and I try to redirect my income into the countryside. This might mean using local shops instead of the supermarkets. It means having work done on my house that directly relates to local skills, such as building a dry stone wall instead of putting up a fence. In my case it means buying local reed for my thatch, instead of the cheaper imports.

All of us who live here – especially those with second homes – can make a big difference economically. Visitors to the area can be encouraged to do more than have a drink and a cream tea. Seeking out farm shops and craft outlets actively supports those people whose livelihood is rooted in the countryside.

We must not make our countryside into a sterile playground. Places thrive when they are more than commuter villages and hotels. Above all, difference, so important in nature, is important to us as human beings. We need imaginative space as well as physical space. We need to see that there are alternatives.

This is one reason why those who seek to ban country sports must be opposed. Rural employment is scarce enough and we cannot lose any of it. I don't want to

RASPING
© Lee Beel

**DAVE HORNBROOK,
TAXIDERMIST**
© John Eveson

live in an homogenised world where we all live in the same way. Country life is different – and if we want to go on enjoying it, we have to let it be different, and that means supporting the countryside as a viable, vibrant community of skills. Let's not turn our countryside into a theme park. Let's not make it about nostalgia for a lost way of life either. The countryside can be our future as well as our past, but only if it is a real place, and not emptied of meaning. Let's maintain

it as a living, emotional, imaginative connection with the earth and ourselves. That is done best when the countryside is a place where people work, as well as a place where people play.

Jeanette Winterson's books are published in 32 countries. Her first novel, *Oranges Are Not The Only Fruit (1985)* won the Whitbread Prize and was successfully adapted for television in 1990.

BEEKEEPER, SUSSEX
© Paul Turner

FOREST OF DEAN FREEMINERS (OPPOSITE)
© David Lloyd
Tradition has it that Edward I granted the miners of the Forest of Dean their status as Freeminers in return for their work in burrowing under the foundations of castles under siege. Their Charter certainly dates back to the 13th century and election as a Freeminer was regarded as an honour.
To be eligible for consideration as a Freeminer, an individual had to be born and living within the Hundred of St Briavels and to have worked for a year and a day in a mine or quarry within the Hundred. Once elected he would ask to be granted a 'gale', a location where he believed iron coal or stone could be found, and would then have to open his mine within five years.
Today there are only a few hundred Freeminers remaining and few of them now cut coal. Their future is threatened as the local hospital has closed and local boys are now born outside the Hundred.

TENT PEG MAKER
© David Lloyd

GOING, GOING, GONE
© Rona Campbell

Food

Clarissa Dickson-Wright

Part of my love for the countryside is that it has always been, for me, a source of food and I love food. Eggs tasted better in childhood when hunted for in the barn where the hens laid, blackberries tasted better picked from autumn hedgerows and milk straight from the cow. As a town child all these things were magical. Today I believe that one aspect of our beleaguered way of life that is progressing is food. True – thousands of people still eat ready meals from supermarkets and devour burgers that we wouldn't feed our dogs; true the governments of the time stitched us up over BSE and the horrors of foot-and-mouth disease (wot no enquiry!) but on the other side of the coin the huge growth of Farmers' Markets is, to me, a constant source of pleasure.

Back in the 1980s when Henrietta Green was the only person carrying the banner of real food, and supermarkets stalked the land like dinosaurs with their horrid unsafe imported food, all seemed lost. Then in 1997 the first Farmers' Market opened in Bristol, and a new era was born. In Winchester I learn the housewives now all plan their dinner parties around the week of the Farmers' Market, rather as our 18th-century ancestors planned them around the date of the full moon, known as the 'parish lantern'.

The impact of the Farmers' Markets is that new schemes are now bringing real food to the public. At Tebay service station on the M6 there are produce shops making real meat, vegetable and dairy products available to the passing public. I recently spent three days in Basingstoke to promote the new permanent food emporium. From Wednesday to Saturday you can buy real meat, fish, vegetables and bread.

Borough Market, which Jennifer and I opened in 1997, makes my heart swell with pride every time I visit it. It is a London market in the best tradition – where pickled lemons from Morocco and Batargo from Spain rubs shoulders with Somerset cider brandy or Cumbrian wild boar. Dear Peter

GENTLEMAN'S FACE
© Martyn Potter

SOW'S EAR
© Martyn Potter

Gott sells bacon that satisfies even my desire for fat bacon, (I am Jack Sprat's wife in such matters). I eat the only burger I will eat from Jan MacCourt, whilst buying his lovely old-breeds meat. Borough Market is where Ginger Pig's photo page shows a group of Saltersgate Farmers, and is where a producer of real chickens will even sell you carcasses for stock.

When my great hero the Duke of Buccleuch began, at the height of BSE, his brilliant scheme of selling his tenants' beef direct to the restaurant market, he shot an arrow whose trail could be seen in all the farm-to-fork meat schemes. For example, I recently met a woman who sells her whole black-faced lamb crop at a premium on the

SHEARER
© Rose Hubbard

ROUND BALES
© Neil Buchan-Grant

internet as 'Heatherlamb'. Hugh Cavendish at Holker, recognising the value the French put on pre-sale lamb, marketed his tenants' entire salt-marsh lamb herd of 1300 beasts at a premium in London and the north west. Schemes such as these are a great help to farmers in these difficult times.

Farmers have always survived because they possess determination, stubbornness and ingenuity. The public, with their urban fear of death, are becoming more aware that what they put in their mouths determines their future

FROZEN CHIPS
© Pauline Rook

health, and that the world from which our Government imports cheap food is increasingly dangerous, unstable and expensive.

I, whose intrinsic good health comes from a lifetime of golden butter, beautiful meat, vegetables grown without supermarket practices and bread baked not steamed (remember the weight comes from the gin lake I consumed) will only be happy when everyone in the nation has joined me. It is now a light I can dimly see through the clouds.

Clarissa Dickson-Wright was born in London but from the age of ten recognised that her soul was happier with country people and country practices. After a lifetime dedicated to good food (and for a lot of it drink as well) she now finds herself in her fifties marching for Liberty & Livelihood, returning to the saddle to hunt and planning the catering for her friends when we all end up behind bars. In her latest TV project – *Clarissa and the Countryman* – she joins her lifelong friend, sheep farmer Sir Johnny Scott, to pay homage to rural Britain, sharing their passion for field sports and traditional country activities.

KNIT ONE, PURL ONE
© Sally Mackenzie

HAPPY PIG
© Pauline Rook

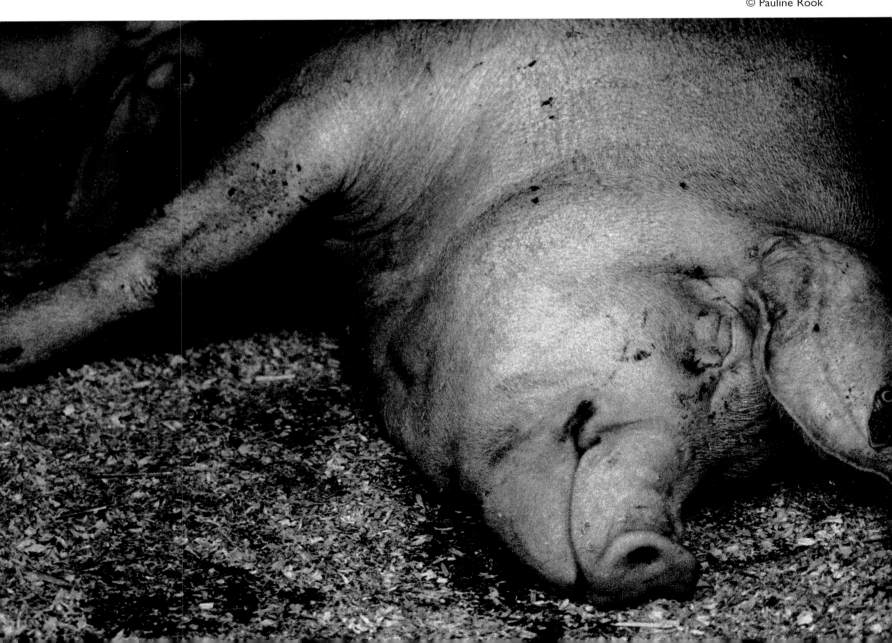

Organic Farming
Caroline Waldegrave

We have a dairy farm in Somerset, which has just become organic after a three year transitional stage. I have been so impressed by the way the Soil Association accredits farms – the occasional spot visits and strict criteria applied make me believe in, and support, food from British organic farms. I don't necessarily believe that organic food tastes any better than non-organic, but there are so many advantages to the environment. We are convinced that there are more butterflies in our fields than before. Better animal husbandry is inevitable where antibiotics are not given as a prophylactic.

FRONT LOADERS
© Thomas Claxton

I was once suspicious that organic farming was a rich man's game, but the considerable government support in the transitional stage and the increased premium once achieved have convinced me – so far – that the sums do add up.

I do, however, think that there is something paradoxical about the amount of imported organic food in our shops. Quite apart from the importance of encouraging local organic farming, organic food (like any other food for that matter) which has travelled half way round the world must be inferior to fresh locally produced products. Henrietta Green, who has done so much to source good quality local food and to encourage the growth in Farmers' Markets, is the champion of this idea, and it seems common sense to me. Those who complain about the damage modern high-production farming has done to British wildlife and the environment, should buy British-grown foods which are being produced in ways that are designed to help conserve our countryside.

Lady Caroline Waldegrave is the co-owner and managing director of Leith's School of Food and Wine and director of Waldegrave Farms Ltd. She is the author of several cookery books including *Leith's Cookery Bible*, *Leith's Guide to Healthy Eating* and *Leith's Easy Dinner Parties*. Caroline Waldegrave received the OBE in 1999 for services to the catering industry, is married to William Waldegrave and has four children.

FOUR CHICKENS
© Thomas Claxton

An Exmoor Hill Farm

Ranulph Fiennes

PLAYTIME
© Thomas Claxton

I have seen some truly beautiful landscapes, from the blue-white expanses of the Antarctic to the desert of the Lost City of Ubar, yet no views have impressed me more than those of Exmoor.

My wife, Ginny, and I have lived on a remote hill farm at the centre of Exmoor National Park for nearly 20 years. At 1,500 feet we are close to its highest point, Dunkery Beacon, with scenery that often includes red deer and wooded combes, wild ponies and stone-faced banks. In late summer, the moor is covered with purple heather; in winter the weather can be hostile — the high land catches clouds from the Atlantic and drives rain horizontally across the bracken.

Ginny farms prize-winning pedigree Aberdeen Angus cattle and Black Welsh Mountain sheep. Both are hardy, disease-resistant breeds that can thrive on the intemperate

ROUNDING UP
© Thomas Claxton

weather in this region. Ginny has 35 breeding cows, all of whom are registered pedigree and are noted for producing choice beef that is high in quality and flavour. All the cows are individually named and many have been with us for years.

I believe that some of the policies made over the past five years will mean the countryside will soon look very different. Without the land management of farmers, huntsmen and gamekeepers, the countryside on Exmoor would quickly revert to gorse and brambles – not ideal for anyone, especially recreational users.

Sir Ranulph Fiennes, writer and explorer, has been at the forefront of polar travel for some 30 years. He now enjoys adventure racing and is a much-sought-after motivational speaker.

WAITING
© Lesley Smith

PIGLET
© Jason Dawson

HOSING DOWN
© Becky Griffiths

BULLOCK IN SUNSET
© Neil Buchan-Grant

To Farm or not to Farm

Frederick Forsyth

G ood, nutritious, fresh British food from British farms on British tables at an affordable price. A pipe dream or a possibility? I believe it is the latter, but only on condition that farmers and Government accept the inevitability of root-and-branch changes. The disasters of BSE and then foot-and-mouth disease were beyond doubt major contributory factors to the virtual collapse of British farming in recent years: 'collapse', that is, as an industry, a career and a job able to offer a fair day's wage for a damned hard day's work. But these were not the real causes; what happened has been on the cards for years. Successive governments, right back to the 1980s, bureaucracy varying from the tyrannical to the spineless, and abysmal farming industry leadership have all played major parts in the

CONTEMPLATION
© Neil Buchan-Grant

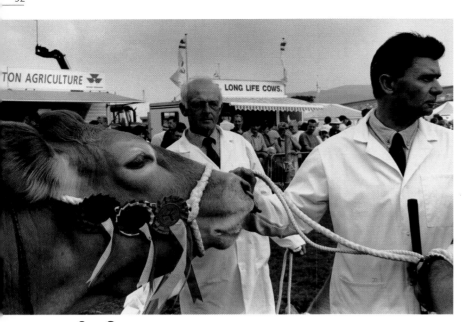

COW SALE
© Becky Griffiths

HAY TURNER (ABOVE)
© Valerie Storer

HOT WORK (BELOW)
© W. P. Andrews

downfall of farming. A recent parliamentary report – the latest of half a dozen – has excoriated all three for making the foot-and-mouth crisis ten times worse than it need have been.

Far too late the British have slowly begun to recognise the link between a viable farming industry and the maintenance of a beautiful landscape... and the reverse. Too late, governments have slowly begun to admit the huge, unpaid task performed by farmers of every kind.

But none has admitted the calamitous effect of the Common Agricultural Policy and its pledges of reform over the past 30 years that have been endlessly refused by the French. None has even tried to rein in the bureaucrats who have piled cost burden after cost burden on British food production while importing mountains of foreign food raised and grown in conditions of animal husbandry and hygiene that would never be tolerated here.

No political party has even attempted to study the installation and assistance of real Farmers' Markets to keep food retailing fresh and local, as our tourists see produce markets prospering in almost every European city and town of any size.

Can it be done here? Oh yes. Will it be done? It must be. Those who love our landscape must simply insist: farming cannot be allowed to die. Native British food must become competitive again.

Frederick Forsyth is probably best known as an author of thrillers (*The Day of the Jackal*, and *The Odessa File* amongst them). Raised in rural Kent 50 years ago he has deep roots in the countryside and now farms (in a small way, he insists) in Hertfordshire. He has repeatedly expressed dismay at what he sees as the slow and unnecessary death of the countryside.

TESTING THE CURDS
© Anthony Fisher

EXODUS
© Masaru Yamada

MOVING SHEEP © Steven Barker
Shepherd Michael Martin moving sheep at Lee Farm
on the Angmening Park Estate, West Sussex.

ROSEMARY
© Martin Elliot

One Woman and her Dog

Katie Cropper

ON THE BOTTLE
© Marilyn Hardman

"Come by! ...Away here! That'll do!" I heard the shepherd's whistles and calls and his subtle voice inflections. I saw the intense concentration of a crouching collie approaching a bustling flock, his ears pricked, his tail rudder-like. I memorised the jargon... 'the lift', 'outrun', 'the fetch', 'drive', 'the course'. Among the flat-capped farmers of the North Wales hill farms a teenage female sheepdog trial enthusiast was an exception – but it had already inspired me more than anything I'd seen and heard in a classroom.

Several years later, on a steep hill in Lancashire, I won my first sheepdog trial with 'Lad'. I was 23, a novice handler, and nervous of letting down my three-legged border collie, still adapting to his disability. But Lad didn't hesitate: black head down, tongue out, eyes focussed, he slunk through the grass, icy-crisp from a late frost. He circled the grey-muzzled swaledale sheep, drove them through the fetch-gate, and into the pen.

AUCTION
© Becky Griffiths

SHEEP RUNNING
© Pete Gelly

BORDER COLLIES
Bred for centuries in Scotland and the border counties to work with sheep, these dogs were used in the first sheepdog trials in 1873 and led to more selective breeding of the type. They are highly intelligent, have great stamina and agility, and respond quickly and eagerly to training.

FARM DOGS
© Dave Dingley

JUMPING ON BOARD
© Thomas Claxton

FARM HANDS
© Jo Hunt

For the past few summers, my three collies and I have gone on tour for two months. We leave our home in Shropshire and travel from show to show – from Norfolk to Turiffe, from Rochester to Moy – in our van with five Herdwick ewes, several ducks, geese, turkeys, a fell pony and my baby daughter, Henrietta. All the animals are used in a show ring to demonstrate my dogs' abilities.

Now, I worry about the future for shepherds. After foot-and-mouth disease, many lost heart and sold up. The Yorkshire Dales, once dotted with sheep and their shepherds, were suddenly full of caravan parks. Sheepdog trials became more commercial, hill-farming sheep a maze of rules, regulations and bureaucracy. Where one tag per sheep used to do, two now seem essential. I'm thankful we don't have to wear suits.

Katie Cropper is Britain's only female winner of the BBC's *One Man and His Dog*, and is a professional shepherdess and sheepdog trialist.

MUCK SPREADING
© Pauline Rook

HIGHLAND CATTLE (OPPOSITE)
© Robert Hughes

MILKING
© Anthony Fisher

Reared on 20 acres

Kate Hoey

FEEDING TIME
© Jo Hunt

My earliest memory is as a four-year-old child walking alone early in the morning up the back lane to the 'far field' to open the trap doors of the henhouses. Then I would stand and watch as dozens of Light Sussex hens spread out to all parts of the field, busily foraging for worms and the other delicious bits they could peck from the soil. It was a perfect start to the day. But I never went alone to shut the hens in at night.

As I grew older I realised why. One night, for some reason, a trap-door was not secured properly. The next morning as I turned the corner near the henhouses I saw the trail of white feathers. A fox had got in. A scene of carnage lay before me. Only two hens were missing but six lay dead — scattered and headless. It was a blow to the family income and a lesson to me. Nature could be very cruel.

PIGS IN THE LAKE DISTRICT
© Robert Hughes

I know that reminiscing about childhood can sometimes be over-romanticised – the cold wet days are forgotten and the sun always seemed to be shining. However, being reared on a small farm of 20 acres in rural County Antrim could not have been a more perfect childhood setting. I only had my older sister to play with so I sought amusement in everything around me. Magic was everywhere – from the secret hideouts we constructed in hedges and trees to the stone under the rickety bridge where I would make my confidential wishes. In the school holidays we would be out in the fields for hours at a time keeping lists of different species of birds we saw and competing to hear the first cuckoo. Indeed the 'first' game was part of growing up. Who could spot the first birds' nest, the first swallow, the first rainbow? My father, who died a couple of years ago just before he

BULLOCK AT DUSK
© David Kirk

CHIPPING, LANCASHIRE
© John Eveson

PLOUGHING

When man discovered that preparing the ground by turning over the soil enabled him to grow better crops this was first done with crude hand-held instruments but, driven by the need for bigger yields, oxen and then horses were harnessed to the plough. Later the development of steam power led to the horse being replaced by the traction engine, which in its turn was superseded by the modern tractor. Ploughing is still the prime job in cultivating the earth, but despite modern technology, the basic design of the plough has remained largely unchanged since medieval times. In early days a champion ploughman would be of great value to the farmer and could expect a better wage. This competitive background led to the introduction of ploughing matches which continue today and are keenly supported at local and national events. The National Ploughing Championships still pay homage to the past with demonstrations of modern equipment as well as traditional ploughing with horses, traction engines and vintage tractors.

PLOUGHING MATCH IN NORFOLK
© Pete Gelly

reached 90, taught me so much about nature. Every week after Sunday school, when I had ambled miles home along country roads, we two would go for a walk by the river which lay at the bottom of our fields to see if anything had changed from the previous week.

There was something so special about the first glimpse of a primrose each spring. It is still my favourite flower and its smell outclasses any other exotic flower on sale in the poshest flower shop in London.

At the age of five I rode my bicycle to the tiny Lylehill primary school. In those days we didn't worry about traffic or child molesters. The journey was uphill but coming home my sister and I would race each other down the hills to see who could free-wheel the longest. The principal was my father's cousin Ben. He would never have lasted in today's world of tests and targets. Yet he instilled in all of us a love of reading and an attitude that you should never put off for tomorrow what could be done better on the day. So, when it was a particularly hot day, we would close our books and take off on a nature ramble, learning the names of different butterflies or quietly listening to the lark soaring above in the cloudless sky. Our farm was organic even though the word was never used in those days. My parents used no fertilisers of any kind and so today the meadows are full of flowers and grasses that are rarely seen in other parts of Northern Ireland. We were almost entirely self-sufficient in the food we ate: my mother made jams and cakes and bread on a daily basis. There were no luxuries, indeed looking back I now know how much my parents sacrificed to ensure that I had the opportunity, when I

GEORGE WITH KID
© Karen Hatch

SHEEP AT DAWN
© David Mason

LAMBS
© Maria Short

passed the 'qualifying' exam, to go to grammar school. My mother would sit late into the night sewing me a new dress so that I would not feel too different from the richer girls I got to know as a teenager. But none of my teenage friends could milk cows or deliver newborn pigs like me. So I did feel different. Some of them had large beautiful houses. We still had a thatched roof and an outside lavatory. What I lacked in material possessions I more than made up for with my knowledge and love of the workings of nature. They have never been forgotten and never will.

Kate Hoey was senior lecturer at Kingsway College from 1976 to 1985 and educational adviser to Arsenal Football Club from 1985 to 1989. Born in Northern Ireland, she is MP for Vauxhall and was the first woman Sports Minister who has proven herself willing to challenge the Government's line on more than one occasion.

The Law of Unintended Consequence

Henry Hobhouse

HORSE BINDER
© David Mason

During the 1930s slump, which affected life in the countryside even more than today's man-made agricultural recession, more people were involved. There were two million farmers, families and workers supported wholly by depressed agriculture. Today, the same people number a tenth of that figure. But peculiar losses due to side effects are even more startling.

In 1939, tractors were only gradually replacing horses for traction. There were still 650,000 horses on farms, needing not only skilled horsemen, but also farriers and harness-makers. There is a strange outcome to this. Horses are fed crushed grain and have less efficient

NORTH LINCOLNSHIRE 1940
© H.A.M. Ltd
Harvesting with one of the first Minneapolis Moline machines to be imported from America.

NORTH LINCOLNSHIRE 1978
© H.A.M. Ltd

J. A. MOLLETT'S FORDSON TRACTOR 1950
© H.A.M. Ltd
Drivers were usually assigned their own
tractors for maintenance reasons.

stomachs than cattle and sheep, so consequently produce rich droppings. The horses in 1939 therefore supported small birds, especially sparrows. The roads were alive with sparrows; all feeding on imperfectly digested corn. Today, the sparrow is an endangered species, partly due to the absence of thousands of horses, each defecating in a sparrow-friendly way. Few bird 'experts' recognise this development, the truth of which can be judged by a visit to a racing stable.

Another by-product of technological change is the virtual abolition of hay or corn ricks. These were the only practical way of storing loose hay and grain-in-sheath. Ricks

CHARLIE NEWBONE RETIRES
© William Mollett

Charlie Newbone spent 50 years on a farm in the North Lincolnshire Wolds. Starting as a boy of 16, he witnessed the transition from heavy horses (opposite top left) through to early Fordson tractors (he can be seen driving one in the middle picture, opposite page), up to present day methods – just one man per machine (opposite bottom left). He is pictured (above) on the day he picked up his final pay-packet when he retired in 1978. By the time he died he had never been to London.

NORTH LINCOLNSHIRE 1955
© H.A.M. Ltd
Harvesting with an early Claas combine.

MODERN AGRICULTURE
Mitsubishi Motors are replacing
more traditional off-road transport © Golly Slater

HORE & SON 1977
© Stephen Cannon

BLACKWELLS: THREE GENERATIONS 2001
© Stephen Cannon

needed wheat straw grown for reed – as it was called – rather than for grain. A great many hazel staves were also needed to peg down thatch in a pattern that shed rain. Hazel was cut (about every 15-25 years) on a coppiced basis and there were thousands of acres of woodland devoted to hazel-husbandry. This huge area in turn provided a wonderful habitat for nightingales. No one knows today how many hectares of coppice-wood (which was also used to light fires) supported nightingales but today nightingales are, like the sparrow, an endangered species. Nowadays, people usually use an oil-based firelighter to light fires, and Dutch barns to store hay. Combine harvesters deliver threshed grain. Straw, if no longer burnt, is baled and stored, but not thatched.

There is a third by-product worth mentioning. When thousands of acres of grassland were ploughed to grow grain during the autumn of 1939, subsequent corn crops sported huge areas of poppies (in winter-sown corn) or

BOB BLACKWELL 1994
© Stephen Cannon

PETERS & SON 1976
© Stephen Cannon

yellow charlock (in spring corn). This was evident even when fields had not been ploughed for a century. We have learnt two lessons. First – some seeds can remain dormant and viable for a long time (even a hundred years). Second – without weedkillers, many fields grow more weeds than grain. When selective weedkillers arrived during World War II, annual weeds disappeared and are hardly known today. 'Flanders' poppies are really only seen in this country around 11th November each year, and are made of plastic or cotton. Both weeds can be observed in their ancient glory in Poland. But not for long, it is said. Polish farmers have been using weedkillers since they were freed from communist control.

Henry Hobhouse is author of *Seeds of Change* and *Seeds of Wealth*, both published by PanMacmillan.

NEWBORN CALF WITH CHICKENS
© Martin Elliot

COW PYRE
© Martin Elliot

MOWN GRASS, HASELBURY PLUCKETT
© Pauline Rook

A Family of Pheasants

Edward Enfield

I always think a pheasant in the garden raises the social tone of the house by a degree or two. Peacocks are all very well, but noisy and a bit over the top. A handsome cock pheasant conveys a certain cachet as he struts about the lawn, which puts one way ahead of the Jones's without any vulgar ostentation.

So when a cock pheasant arrived, naturally I took steps to feed him so that he would stay around. He quickly grasped that he was on to a good thing and brought his hen friend along, and we would watch the pair of them wandering about the garden as if they owned it. Then the hen seemed to make herself scarce, until one day I came across her about two yards from the front door, right up against the wall of the house, nestling among some rockroses and looking rather nervous at the thought that I had spotted her. I tiptoed away, and when I next noticed her I found that she had been sitting on ten eggs. We would pass and re-pass a few feet from her nose; the postman and the newspaperman came and went; she never moved. A number of visitors came to look at her but she sat as firm as a rock and looked right back at them.

ENGLISH HARE
© John Eveson

EAGLE OWL
© Tony Shaw

FROG IN WATER
© Mark Fairhurst

BROWN HARE
© David Mason

Although not native to Britain, hares were introduced at least 2,000 years ago for hunting purposes and feed mainly on grass, roots, bark and the produce of farms and gardens. Unlike rabbits they live in the open, and rely on their keen senses and great speed to evade predators.

Some of their elaborate mating rituals in the spring have led to the phrase 'as mad as a March hare'. When a female is rebuffing an amorous male, the pair often appears to be taking part in a boxing match.

A major survey in the late 1990s estimated the current population at just 750,000, unevenly distributed with the highest concentration in East Anglia. Concern over declining numbers led to the inclusion of the brown hare on the list of vulnerable species for which a UK Biodiversity Action Plan was written in the early 1990s.

BIRD ON WIRE
© E. M. Liddon

My pheasant-shooting neighbour explained to me that when the eggs hatched she would take the chicks to a supposed place of safety, whereupon magpies would eat them. "I'm not having that", I said, and built a sort of aviary round her out of old wire shelving. She looked decidedly anxious, but stayed put.

In the course of time, eight eggs hatched. The chicks emerged from under the hen and rushed around like mice, falling in the water bowl or sitting in the chick crumbs. They learned to fly surprisingly quickly and performed tiny aerobatics in the aviary. When I pushed some bean sticks in for perches, they sat on them at once. All in all, as pheasants go, they seemed quite intelligent.

When they were six weeks old they were pronounced to be magpie-proof. We had a large, fox-proof, unoccupied chicken run at the bottom of the garden so we clipped their wings and moved them. When their wings grew back they started to fly out, so my neighbour suggested I should make pop-holes in the fence so that they could pop back. They were not intelligent about the pop-holes, preferring to walk up and down the wrong bit of the fence in a despairing manner, and I spent some time shooing them back.

Still, it all settled down. They came and went. There were five cocks and three hens, plus the mother, and having

FROSTED LEAVES
© Jo Riddle

INSECT IN BERRIES
© Chris Mole

got to this number in one season I began to wonder if, by arithmetical progression, I should be knee-deep in pheasants in the course of a very few years. Nature, though, took a hand.

One morning I went down and there was not a pheasant to be seen. There was no blood or feathers, so the fox had not got in. Perhaps some sly poacher had come in the night and collared the lot? I went to report this alarming development to my neighbour and from his garden I saw them, strung out like schoolgirls going to church in a crocodile, marching along behind their mother away from home.

"Never mind" I thought, "they will come back to feed," but they did not. I used to meet them occasionally when I went for a walk, or see them crossing the road, but they never returned. I thought it was a little casual the way they just cleared off like that, but I suppose they could hardly form up to say goodbye.

The original cock pheasant showed no interest in his family, and never came near the aviary. But I am pleased to say that he is back, strutting about the garden, raising the social tone and enhancing the value of the property. He has not brought a hen with him but he makes encouraging noises, so who knows? Perhaps we are about to go round again, in which case the spot among the rockroses is vacant and I have the mobile aviary at the ready.

After completing a degree in Classics at Oxford and national service in Germany, Edward Enfield spent five years in the Far East. On his return to England he worked for West Sussex County Council. He writes a regular column in *The Oldie* magazine and has forged what he calls 'a little mini-career' in journalism, radio and television. His latest book *Greece on my Wheel* is a mixture of anecdote, history and gleanings from earlier travellers to Greece.

LOG PILE
© Terry Greenwood

EARLY MORNING FROST
© Brian Jordan

SWAN IN A QUARRY
© Susan Leedale

THREE SWANS
© Martin Pickles
Moorgreen Nature Reserve, near Finchampstead,
Berkshire, on a spring morning.

FAMILY OUTING
© Martin Pickles

SWAN CHARGE
© Martin Pickles

BEECH
© Jane Body

FORGET-ME-NOTS
© Jane Body

COW PARSLEY
© Jane Body

COWSLIPS
© Jane Body

Discovery
Philip Mould

FROGSPAWN
© E. M. Liddon

There appears to be no-one alive to tell me why the Slumpet bears its name. Or if there is, I have yet to meet them. I began asking questions about a year ago when I found it on a map of the land around our house in Oxfordshire marked with early field names.

To reach the Slumpet I first had to trespass by foot across a small marsh and stream containing the remains of an ancient sheep wash. Once committed, I continued further down a shallow valley which led to an isolated field called Inoculation – a Black Death site of now forgotten purpose. Here the atmosphere began palpably to change.

This lonely enclosure is bordered by a disused railway line, which is now as silent as the rest of this hidden tract that drops in stages towards a boggy field of sedge to which I now headed. The air became detectably softer, the temperature lower, as I descended the valley. The further down I travelled, the greater became the sensation of having entered a channel of nature that was dislocated from its surroundings. Its remoteness conspired with the lengthening shadows to create a heady sense of walking back, rather than forward.

At its bottom, across from a field of marsh, stood the bristling profile of the Slumpet – a two-acre strip of ancient woodland, which by dint of its seclusion, had miraculously survived the assaults of agriculture for perhaps a thousand years or more.

WINTER SKY
© Patrick Newnham

PAIR OF LUNGS
© Phil Bowman

LAKE DISTRICT
© David Stephenson

I had been warned it was a strange place, and intrepidly pushing my way in through perimeter branches I began to feel that the Slumpet had evolved to resist humans. Paths or tracks were absent. Navigation was only possible by way of green light filtering through the canopy, mapping out irregular patches of clearing. Blocking my strides were stringy spring plants, adapted anaemics with lanky, overly-visible stems that strenuously stretched for the light in attitudes of worship. My discovery took place as I reached the Slumpet's heart. As often with things wild and ancient, at first it conspired with its surroundings to hide from view. Only after a few moments of hard observation came the

BURNHAM OVERY
© Paul Bennett

BURNHAM OVERY STAITHE
© Paul Bennett

HORSE AND POPPIES, NORFOLK
© Geoff du Feu

SPRING
© David Stephenson

realisation that the gentle change of tone and shape around my feet was the edge of a long colony, an unravelling and twisting shoal that followed the stream's edge, its delicate mass carpeting tree roots as it spread from view into the recesses of the clearing. Seen only before in my plant books, I had stumbled upon a thrilling treasure.

The reasons why this scarce and magical plant – which was described as rare even in the 19th century –

bears the name Herb Paris, are obscure. An historic reference to Paris of Troy, say some. The origins of its other common name, True Love Knot, are less conjectural. The ancient cross-shaped knot shared between lovers, referred to by Chaucer, closely resembles its cruciform whorl of leaves from which springs a single purple flower on a slender stalk. Spider-like stamens add to its bizarre appearance, giving Herb Paris the look of something

DAWN
© David Stephenson

prehistoric or unearthly, but also beautiful, suited to the arresting woodcuts of Tudor apothecaries who credited it with the powers to 'repress the force of poison'.

To me the Slumpet could not have delivered a greater reward. This rare piece of living antiquity in its medieval hide-out embodied everything that is uplifting, indeed central, to our national heritage – as indivisible from our culture as our listed stately homes, our Raphaels and our excavated Roman hoards. It is heritage that remains despite, rather than because of human intervention – a lonely and portentous survivor of man's adversity to nature

Philip Mould is an art dealer, author and broadcaster. He is also chairman of Plantlife International, the leading wild plant conservation charity. Since 1988 he has been the honorary adviser on art to the House of Commons and the House of Lords.

ROBIN © Mark Fairhurst

Robins first appeared on Christmas cards as a representation of Victorian postmen, who wore red tunics and were known as 'redbreasts'. The robin is Britain's national bird, chosen by the International Council for Bird Preservation in 1961. Belonging to the thrush family, these predominantly woodland birds can be heard singing all year round, feeding on scraps, berries and insects from the ground. They have a trusting nature and interact well with humans, but are aggressive towards other robins when defending their territory. It is not uncommon to find robins attacking red objects which they perceive to be a threat.

ENTWINED. KNIGHTHAYES COURT, DEVON
© Lyn Cole

Dangerous Hedgehogs
Duff Hart-Davis

On an island crowded with 60 million people, our less successful wild creatures need all the help they can get if they are to survive. What is more, many of them are getting that help, and an enormous amount of conservation work is being carried out: otters, dormice and capercaillie, to name but three species, are all the recipients of extensive human effort.

Take capercaillie. These magnificent great grouse, as big as slender turkeys, became extinct in Britain late in the 18th century. Reintroductions in the 1830s established them again in Scotland, and they bred so well that they became a menace to foresters, nipping off thousands of pine shoots. Now, though, they are once more in serious decline, with probably fewer than 1,000 birds left in the whole country. Several large estates in Scotland are doing everything they can to encourage the remaining population.

At Abernethy, on Speyside, for instance, the Royal Society for the Protection of Birds took the unpopular step of drastically culling red deer in and around the ancient Caledonian forest, so that the bilberry and heather on which capercaillie depend for food and shelter could become more luxuriant. The Society also began, dropped and re-started a policy of culling predators – principally foxes and grey crows – which take the eggs and chicks of ground-nesting birds.

While capercaillie hang in the balance, peregrine falcons have made a powerful comeback from the nadir of the 1960s, when the indiscriminate use of noxious pesticides reduced them to a low ebb. Again, this is the result of determined efforts, by the RSPB and others, to secure legal protection, to have poisonous chemicals banned, to deter egg-thieves, and so on. Another major success has been the reintroduction of the red kite: in 1989 young birds brought from Spain and Sweden were secretly released at Wormsley, the late Sir Paul Getty's estate in the Chilterns, and now, with further reinforcements, they have repopulated much of the country.

Bungalows designed specifically for bats are being built at huge expense. Military bulldozers clear areas the size of football pitches on Salisbury Plain so that stone curlews, which like nesting with plenty of room round them, can feel

FLEDGLINGS
© Claire Thorpe

at home. Artificial nesting boxes are set up in numerous Midland counties to furnish ever-dozy dormice with safe refuges.

Otters, meanwhile, have made a spectacular return to strength, in direct response to human effort expended on their behalf. With the clean-up of inland waterways, the provision of artificial holts and the restoration of suitable habitat along river banks, numbers have climbed back to the 4,000 mark, and most of the animals' former haunts have been reoccupied. In Kent, a colony of Norwegian beavers has been established – the first to live semi-wild in Britain for 400 years – and another is planned for Scotland. Conservationists are also pursuing schemes for reintroducing wolves into the Scottish Highlands.

Interest in wild creatures is intense. The Wildlife Trusts are flourishing as never before, and hundreds of volunteers turn out to help with counts organised by bodies like the Mammal Trust and the British Trust for Ornithology.

Of course, not everyone is in favour of giving wildlife unlimited rope. Most people are prepared to kill a rat. Foresters loathe grey squirrels because, by stripping bark, they damage or kill trees by the thousand. Even the gentlest of gardeners rebel against magpies when they see them choking down the eggs and chicks of songbirds. Is it not sensible to keep such pests to a reasonable level, culling them by humane means?

The same applies to badgers. Few animals stir up more animosity than Brock, who is now so heavily protected by law that it is an offence to take action against him, even if his digging undermines a building. Brock has a huge army of supporters, in the 80,000 members of the National Federation of Badger Groups, who resist all attempts by the government to reduce his numbers. Yet dairy farmers hate him, and keep demanding culls, because they know that he carries bovine tuberculosis, and almost certainly passes the disease to cattle.

The long-term solution to the problem must lie in the development of a vaccine to control TB in both badgers and cattle, and in more efficient management. The irony of the present situation is that some 50,000 badgers are being killed on roads every year – one about every seven and a

INTIMATE TRUNKS. KNIGHTHAYES COURT, DEVON
© Lyn Cole

CUMBRIA
© David Stephenson

half minutes – and there is nothing anyone can do to stop the slaughter.

Finally – hedgehogs. Harmless though they look, they can be very destructive – for instance they destroy sea-bird colonies by eating their eggs. Yet hedgehogs have a tremendous human fan-club. Early in 2003, when Scottish Natural Heritage announced that it was proposing to trap and kill 5,000 of them on the Hebridean islands of North and South Uist and Benbecula, there was not merely a national but an international outcry, fwith demands that the animals be saved and transported to alternative locations on the mainland. The cull for this year closed at the end of May, after only 66 hedgehogs had been killed, a little over a quarter of SNH's target of 200. Animal rights' groups apparently rescued 140 hedgehogs and transferred them to the mainland.

Again, it is a question of managing wildlife sensibly – and surely SNH is right to decide that the dunlin, redshank, snipe, plovers and oystercatchers which have inhabited the islands for generations should have priority over a species introduced only 30 years ago.

Duff Hart-Davis is the author of some 35 books, including *Fauna Britannica* and *Monarchs of the Glen*, a history of deer-stalking in the Scottish Highlands. From 1986 to 2001 he contributed the 'Country Matters' column to *The Independent*. He lives in a 17th-century farmhouse on the Cotswold escarpment.

FEEDING WASP
© Mark Fairhurst

DORMICE

The word dormouse probably comes from the French verb 'dormir' meaning 'to sleep'. Weighing about 20 grams and measuring less than 7 cm, the common dormouse is a strictly nocturnal animal and spends about three quarters of its life asleep. Mainly found in southern England, they have been in steady decline for decades due threats such as habit fragmentation and climate change.

RIP VAN & WINKLE © Sam Clark
Three dormice found hibernating in Somerset 2003

Gossip
Daisy Waugh

From my noisy, polluted, anonymous desk here in London W12, I make numerous telephone calls to my country-dwelling friends. For lack of any of my own, I collect their gossip from the village. It's a harmless hobby, and very useful for my line of work:

> I know her mother eloped with the school dinner lady.
> I know he's been to jail for fraud.
> I know her husband's going bust.
> I know he dropped a German tourist 30 foot into a river and very nearly killed him.
> I know they set fire to their own B&B and got a lot of money out of insurance.
> I know he starved half his pigs to death.
> I know she ruined their last party by firing a shotgun at his head.
> I know their goat's decapitated body washed up in a dustbin bag on the banks of the river Exe.
> I know it was witchcraft and I know which one's the witch.
> I know he likes teenage boys.
> I know she's an alcoholic.
> I know he's dying... And
> I know they like to be naked when the news is on.

All of this is true. By which I mean, of course, all of this I have heard. Rumour has it.

But there are no rumours where I live. No clues. No time for conversation at all. In London W12, we're either very busy or we're very shy, and besides we all speak different languages. Which is nice. Isolation and mystery guaranteed. Between the telephone calls I gaze out of my window and can watch an endless stream of enigmatic figures go by. Some of them I have watched for years; some of them I actually smile at; some of them, I strongly suspect, live in the house next door.

I'm not complaining. Far from it. Because although I live to hear of my country cousins' boundless peccadillos

Capel Horticultural Society Spring Show
© Paul Styles

VILLAGE FÊTES

The village fête is a traditional part of rural life, with its roots going back to the Middle Ages or beyond. One survivor from earlier days is the maypole which was originally a pagan fertility symbol. The young girls of the village would dance round the pole to celebrate the return of spring and ensure the fertility of the land. Succeeding the pagan fairs the village fête became a religious event in celebration of the patron saint of the village, and in medieval England the churches brewed and sold ales for the occasion. Later the church authorities separated the fête from the religious occasion. The village fête today still retains its old links with the church, with the event often used to fund-raise for the church. Dancing round the maypole or Morris dancing may still be seen side by side with more commercial ventures such as tombolas, raffles, cake stalls, bouncy castles or coconut shies.

HACKING OUT
© Philiy Page

BONFIRE NIGHT
© Chris Mole

BRUNSWICK
© Martin Elliot

and failings, my own I prefer to keep private. So when my neighbours (if neighbours they are) hear our gunfire, our pig grunts or the lash of our whips, I know they won't call the police or their best friends, or even bother to put a glass to the wall. Perhaps if one of us is dying incredibly loudly they might notice it enough to turn their tellies up.

Unfriendly? Obviously. And thank God for that.

Daisy Waugh is a novelist. Her most recent best-sellers are *The New You Survival Kit* and its sequel *Ten Steps to Happiness* published by HarperCollins.

SUMMER FAIR, WITHAM
© Chris Chapman

BIRD BOX
© Paul Styles

LONELY NEW FOREST POSTBOX
© Margaret Penwarden
Alone in the heart of the beautiful Blackmore Vale this isolated postbox, on its ivy-covered support, provides a convenient haven for indigenous wildlife, as well as an essential means of communication.

PORTCHESTER POSTBOX
© Margaret Penwarden
Portchester, Hampshire was once an important staging post for London-bound mail coaches with innkeepers providing tankards of ale and fresh horses. This former inn is now a private dwelling but the postbox remains in use.

POSTBOX ON POST
© Margaret Penwarden
Notwithstanding its slight subsidence problem, this leaning postbox in Upper Charminster, Dorset is strategically placed in front of the village notice board.

The Postmaster

Nicholas Crane

shton under Hill: with the turning of the season came the turning of the soil. The stubble fields were being sliced and folded into moist clods that shone like cut liver. The body of the earth sweated a slight mist. The field paths I followed from Cropthorne wandered south through these vapours towards the solidifying form of Bredon Hill. Sadly, the viewpoint that William Cobbett described as 'a richer spot than is to be seen in any other country of the world' lay just the wrong side of the 99 grid line. Beneath Bredon straggled Ashton under Hill.

The sub-postmaster spoke bitterly of the way the village was going. 'The pub's only just surviving. Rent increases, all that jazz. The shop closed 12 months ago; the supermarkets in Evesham did it.' He described in incredulous tones how villagers had asked him to sell raffle tickets in order to raise money to buy a minibus so that elderly inhabitants could shop in Evesham. 'Incredible.' He shook his head. 'They really couldn't see that the raffle tickets they wanted me to sell would kill my own business.'

'People don't even bother to come here for stamps now. They'll buy a book of first-class stamps from the garage while they're filling up, rather than walk 20 yards to my post office. Everything here depends on wheels. You won't get a job without wheels.'

Otherwise, he said, the village was doing all right. It had a cricket and football team. A tennis club. The Bredon Hillbillies were down to play a gig and line-dancing classes could be taken in the village hall.

'Is it a happy village?'

'There's not a lot of animosity,' he said. 'A little tittle-tattle. The usual.'

Chris performed the tasks expected of a village post office: keeping the chimney-sweep list and the phone numbers of reliable plumbers. 'I do the box office for the amateur dramatics too,' he added. 'I do it for the village, for nothing. But people still ring me up and are rude.'

As I was leaving, he handed me a leaflet issued by the National Federation of Sub-Postmasters headed BEWARE! The leaflet described how the Department of Social Security wanted to pressurise people into having their pensions and benefits paid directly into their personal

POSTBOXES

The pillar box, first painted red in 1874 (and re-painted at least once every 3 years) is now recognised as a national treasure by English Heritage, who aim to ensure that they cannot be demolished. First appearing 150 years ago, there are now some 115,000 postboxes in the UK. Apertures were originally marked with 'Town' and 'Country'. Previously, in rural communities, a person had to wait at the roadside in all weathers for the arrival of the Post Office Messenger, or travel a long way to reach a 'receiving house.' The oldest postbox in use on mainland Britain stands at Barnes Cross, Bishop's Caundle, in Dorset.

POSTBOX IN NEW FOREST
© Margaret Penwarden

accounts rather than allowing them the choice of collecting them at the local post office, then warned that 'thousands of post offices may have to close'. The leaflet's last bullet-point read: 'The community role of the local sub-post office is very important. It offers services, it is a vital part of a community, it encourages more people to shop locally.'

It was true, but like all the other services that helped make rural communities function, nobody wanted to pay the extra premium.

Nicholas Crane is author of *Two Degrees West: A Walk Along England's Meridien* published by Penguin Books.

BATTLE FACE
© Martin Elliot

BIRD WOMAN
© Martin Elliot

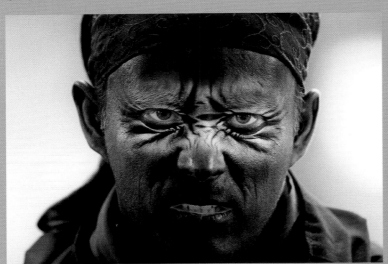

VILLAGE PAPER BOY
© Ian Montgomery

A Bishop's Village
The Right Reverend Jim Thompson, former Bishop of Bath and Wells

As a priest and then a bishop, I lived for 22 years in east London with my wife and family. The dying Royal Docks were included within my first parish, East Ham. The second was a new town called Thamesmead, which consisted of 19 tower blocks. While we were there, 30,000 people moved in. Finally, when I became Bishop of Stepney we moved to Commercial Road E1, and remained in Tower Hamlets for 13 years.

Becoming the Bishop of Bath and Wells and moving to Somerset was therefore a huge change in our lives. In retirement we live in a village on Exmoor where I took up the post of an honorary assistant curate.

I found the contrast between the deeply urban and the deeply rural staggering. I experienced the wide gulf that exists both in environment and in culture between a vast conurbation and a village with its surrounding countryside. This divide is also reflected in the political map, which often means that the two main parties lack the experience and the commitment to serve areas that are not their heartlands.

We have more time to think about these contrasts now, and to see the village as neighbours, churchgoers, horse lovers and in-comers. In it we have found refreshment from the hardest features of the inner city – alienation from nature; the break-up of communities; the brutalising of some of the worst estates, homelessness and other sorts of poverty. I could also pay great tribute to the courage, the kindness, the laughter, the cosmopolitan life and multiracial experience of the inner city, which enriched us.

The first impact of country life for me was the beauty of the environment – the moors, streams and coastland. The remains of the ancient forest provide shelter and daytime concealment for the wild red deer. The sky at night is not obscured by the city lights. The air is pure and the horizon lends space and depth to the eye in every direction.

The community also brings its blessing. There are occasionally feuds and gossip, but the relationships are mostly positive and a continuous source of enrichment. They create a real sense of belonging for people who can be isolated in the wilds. The pub, the post office, the school, the church and the village shop are all places where people congregate.

Many people meet at the hunts as well. On September evenings it sometimes appears that most of the village is watching from a sunny hillside, while the foxes' evasions allow time to chat. Churches are now mostly joined together, and in many cases this has brought villages closer as co-operation and shared worship can lead to greater combined resources.

In the forbidding silence of the underground in London, I occasionally think of how much more the small, warm, spontaneous rural community can offer to the individual. However, there are real problems in the countryside as well which are given very full coverage in the media – the near despair of hill farmers, the serious need for affordable housing, the withdrawal of precious services, inadequate provision for young people's social life, and discrete rural poverty. But it is also important to recognise how much of God's wonderful world the village and the countryside give to the people who live there.

Having lived in both extreme urban and rural areas we hope they will understand each other better, and recognise their mutual dependence and realise that they have great and varied resources to offer each other.

The Right Reverend Jim Thompson trained as a chartered accountant. The Royal Tank Regiment and Cambridge led on to the priesthood. He was in East London for 22 years, as Rector of Thamesmead and Bishop of Stepney, before becoming Bishop of Bath and Wells. He very sadly died in September 2003 shortly after this article was written.

DUCK RACE
© Julie Dennis

PETAL BEARERS, MAY QUEEN FESTIVAL, HAYFIELDS, DERBYSHIRE
© Tom Taylor

EVENING CRICKET MATCH AT ANSTY, SUSSEX
© Chris Mole

A Man of Kent

Sandy Gall

I first went abroad as a novice foreign correspondent for Reuters in 1953, almost exactly 50 years ago. It was the first of many journeys to cover coups, wars and disasters of one kind or another in many parts of the world – Africa, the Middle East, Asia, the Far East.

I soon discovered that wars were an inseparable part of a foreign correspondent's job.

Very often the call of duty meant leaving Britain at the best seasons of the year, in spring, summer or autumn – I did not mind so much in winter – or when there was a family occasion, school holidays, sports days, a visit to Glyndebourne or some other excitement. The wrench of leaving was balanced of course by the excitement of the assignment.

Over the years, these departures, nearly always sudden and unexpected, became the pattern of one's life. Each was a miniature voyage of exploration. Some, like Cyprus, were almost pure pleasure, and despite the fighting between Greek and Turkish Cypriots, never seemed particularly dangerous. Others, like the Congo, were frightening, unpredictable – the heat, humidity and general anarchy adding several dimensions of horror. Others again, like Vietnam, were countrywide wars, involving a million troops or more, where you could feel dwarfed and lost.

It was on my way back from one of these assignments, as we approached the English coast over the for once sparkling North Sea that I suddenly saw the light. It was a beautiful day – it must have been high summer – and fragments of Shakespeare came into my mind; 'this scepter'd isle... This precious stone set in the silver sea... This blessed plot, this earth, this realm, this England'... I realised almost with the shock of conversion just how truly, deeply and immensely fortunate I was – we were – to live in a country like this. I had come from somewhere where the land was brown and parched, Africa perhaps, and below us as we descended to Gatwick, my favourite airport, the countryside was an ancient tapestry of greens and yellows, some pale, others – copses perhaps – so dark as to be almost black, with the occasional blue flash of a swimming pool. I looked as always for my own oast house, surrounded by fields but, as always, failed to find it.

This feeling of wonder has always remained with me, and is always sharper of course if I have just come back from some hellhole. In 1972, about a dozen of us were the involuntary guests of mad Idi Amin in Uganda. It was the aftermath of the deportation of Uganda's Asian community, all 40,000 of them, and we too were deported. I had been in a military barracks where they boasted an execution cell – luckily not required. We were flown home by what was then British Caledonian but instead of landing at Gatwick, we were diverted because of fog to Manchester, but I did not mind.

Soon afterwards I would journey through the Kent and Sussex lanes to Glyndebourne on the South Downs. I think we watched the *Marriage of Figaro*. That night, the first sip of picnic champagne, surrounded by old-fashioned roses in full bloom, restored my sense of almost unbelievable good fortune. As did more simple things like the taste of Kentish strawberries, and my own new potatoes.

The magic still works although the palate may be slightly jaded now. Earlier this summer, I spent three weeks in Afghanistan where life is harsh and the landscape, although beautiful, often savage. Soon after returning we went to Cambridge and stayed at Madingley Hall, a medieval pile once rented by Queen Victoria as rooms for the undergraduate Prince of Wales. The garden was a revelation of what a classic English garden ought to be. I was enchanted by the old roses and clematis, the rich, weed-free soil and the effortless sense of perfection.

And, dare I say it, my own clematis, the Marie Boisselot and Lasurstern have been superb this year and as I write the Perle d'Azur is at the height of its Giotto-blue perfection.

God Bless 'This land of such dear souls, this dear, dear land.' [King Richard II]

Sandy Gall was born in Penang, Malaysia, in 1927 and educated in Scotland at Glenalmond and Aberdeen University. He was a foreign correspondent for Reuters, 1953-1963, and a war correspondent and newscaster for ITN 1963-1992, covering Vietnam, Cambodia, China, the Middle East, Africa and Afghanistan. His last two major assignments for ITN were the Gulf War (1991), where he was the first journalist to report from liberated Kuwait, and the fall of Kabul (1992). He was awarded the Sitara-I-Pakistan by President Zia in 1985, the Lawrence of Arabia Memorial Medal by the Prince of Wales in 1987 and the CBE in 1988. He and his wife Eleanor have four children and live in Penshurst, Kent.

Snubbed by a Shopkeeper

Julian Fellowes

I think it was Agatha Christie's Miss Marple who remarked that the advantage of living in Saint Mary Mead was not that the village was far removed from real life. On the contrary, it was that all variations of the human struggle were represented on a modest scale within its boundaries. And it is surely true that anyone wishing to 'get away from it all' had better avoid residence in an English village and make instead for the Arctic Circle.

The unsuspecting townie who has spent so many years protected from any involvement in his community, ignorant of the troubles and even the identity of his next-door neighbours, will find himself, on moving to his rural idyll, flung into the heart of fiercely prosecuted goals and feuds.

He may dream of neutrality once he has arrived on this battlefield but it will not be allowed him, even though whichever team he chooses in the fray will bring the enmity of half the new neighbours in its wake. The planning permission for that field on the edge of the envelope, the proposed new use of those empty farm buildings or simply whether or not the vicar is a pest... Let it be never so minor an issue, the moment he takes one side he risks a snub in the shop while the other will bring whispered murmurs or a hostile glance as he orders a pint in the pub. I can only imagine that many first-time country dwellers must wonder why they ever exchanged the peace and quiet of Oxford Street in the sales for this sea of contention.

MAENCLOCHOG
© Ian Jebbett

SHAMROCK CAFÉ
© Lucy Mellor

Hartland is an isolated village on the north Devon coast, 15 miles from the nearest town and supermarket. People don't go out of the village very often, so they do most of their shopping locally. Hartland supports five small shops, three pubs and a fish-and-chip shop. One of these shops is The Shamrock Café — a fruit-and-veg, bits-and-bobs and chip-shop. It is family run and Pearl, a grandmother, does a lot of the work. It's a bit seedy and old-fashioned but the service is very friendly and Pearl knows everyone's name. If the shop is lacking anything she has in her own larder she'll get it from there.

But of course that is not the whole of it, for what village life boasts that so much of urban life has lost is its human scale. It is not just the community or their houses that are of a size that seems comprehensible to us, but their problems too. The residents of a village will know — or at least know of — almost every other inhabitant and they will consequently understand the issues that underpin the quarrels and the campaigns. It is easy, surrounded by the roar of London or New York, to feel that the forces governing us are wrapped in an impermeable mist and that nothing we can say or do will have any effect on them. The best we can hope for as we fit another burglar alarm or lock another garage is to be left alone, to be spared as the thuggish elements pass by. But a village does not, and cannot afford to, tolerate the isolationist. The world of the village is still a world where the individual voice must be heard, where the individual wish can be respected, where the individual dream may be pursued. And in our increasingly faceless and heartless epoch, it seems to me that the sense of being able to make a difference is well worth a snub in the village shop.

Julian Fellowes, writer, actor and director, played the incorrigible Kilwillie in the BBC's *Monarch of the Glen*. He won an Oscar in 2002 for the screenplay of *Gosford Park*. He and his wife, Emma, have recently bought a house in Dorset.

DONKEY LADY OF CLOVELLY
©Victoria Hunt

From Yeovil to Yorkshire

Ian Botham

When I was 16, I worked at Lord's Cricket Ground, and lived in London for a year and a half. It was the only time I've lived in London. I found it impersonal: a world away from Yeovil, the small town in Somerset where I grew up, and where I knew nothing but open air and empty roads and fishing the river Yeo in summer.

Now that I'm older and living with my own family in North Yorkshire, I take rural existence less for granted and am constantly inspired by it. I spend so much time in aeroplanes, hotels or foreign cities that when I have time off, all I want to do is to be at home in the country. My grandchildren spend their days in the fields, or on their quad bikes, coming home to feed the pheasant chicks in the woods and scanning the lake for fish in the evenings. Local loyalty is strong: we know if we are away that someone will keep an eye on our home. I have never found the same sense of community concern in cities.

There is so much that is beautiful in our countryside, but I believe strongly that we do need to understand that so much of it is managed by the people who live and work in it. They keep the banks of rivers clean and build up fish stocks. They look after fields, hedges and woods. Those who don't understand the British countryside need to see it operate throughout the changing seasons, see it managed by people who have intricate knowledge of it and have spent generations creating an extraordinary natural landscape.

Ian Botham OBE was a world-class cricketer who captained England 1980-81. His ability with either bat or ball was best seen in the 1982 series against Australia, when he effectively won two matches single-handed. His recreations include shooting, salmon and trout fishing.

CROCK OF GOLD
© John Eveson

VILLAGE TEAM
© Peter Glenser

OYSTER FARMING
© William de la Hey

Coastal Life

The Sea, The Sea
Simon Schama

My earliest childhood memory is of my father standing on the other side of the French doors, which led from our grandiose sitting room out into the garden, lighting fireworks for Guy Fawkes' night. Beyond there were Catherine wheels and Roman candles but for the four-year-old me there were just sparklers. The next memory, though, is of the sea, infinite, steely grey, with washes of green, and the smell of it too, iodine strong with wracks of weed, which draped the beaches between Southend and Leigh-on-Sea.

It was one of my father's intermittent periods of prosperity, handsome enough to allow him to buy the big

OYSTER FARMING

Large European native oysters were eaten across Scotland during their heyday in 18th and 19th centuries. They were so plentiful and cheap that many recipes demanded up to 60 oysters per dish. The beds became polluted and over-fished, and were almost wiped out by mid-20th century. Their revival is down to farming commercially-cultivated — predominantly gigas — oysters although some farms are now experimenting with natives in sheltered sea lochs on the Scotland's west coast. Lochs must have shelter and be pollution-free with a rich supply of natural nutrients. The young seeds are placed in mesh bags which are put on wooden trestles at the low-water mark, or on plastic trays stacked on the sea bed. They are usually harvested after two to three summers' feeding.

BRIGHTON: FISHING BOAT
© Chris Mole

COCKLES
© Jon Crane

seaside house on the Thames Estuary, complete with sunken garden and winsome statuary, and a small fountain in which my Lithuanian-Jewish grandpa would deposit his yellow-Russian dog-ends. The salty damp clung to the washing lines (for this was the late 1940s and early 1950s) and everything about that world was, for a nosey child, glorious. I roamed the broad mudflats, bucket in hand looking for small crabs inhabiting a scuttling rock-pool universe. Just occasionally I would transfer this world to our bathroom, forgetting my sister's bath-time until reminded by her screams of pain and fury.

Many years later I read L.P. Hartley's *The Shrimp and the Anemone* and dimly recognised the secretive world of seaside beaches, the freedom and danger that came with undress. Years later still, I read Paul Theroux's account of exploring the seaside perimeter of Britain and didn't at all recognise the melancholy of the places he trudged through, ridiculous and uncomfortably depressed, like a man wearing

COCKLES II
© Jon Crane

brogues along a stretch of Essex shingle. Perhaps I was lucky to have my childhood at a time before there were package holidays to the Costa del Sol; for Southend was humming with delicious wickedness; oozing, shrieking pink rock that stuck to one's teeth; chips to soak up the Sarson's Malt Vinegar so that they became flabby and dissolved into a kind of potato goo. I couldn't get enough. The Kurzaal amusement park with small animals going round and round (I was partial to the duck) and the pier were still places of raucous beauty and always there was that endless, tawny-grey stretch of mud heading off to who knows where, Belgium? China?

And the people who made their living in this world seemed to be universally benevolent hordes of uncles and aunties; from the donkey-ride men to the bus conductors on the cream-coloured double-deckers with the open tops, one of whom fed me furtive Smarties. Today I suppose he would get arrested for same.

Leigh-on-Sea, not far away from our Chalkwell house was a place of semi-forbidden delight, since there were still shrimp boats and cockle- and winkle-sheds and from them issued aromas of deeply un-Kosher beauty which I remember inhaling with intense longing so that they filtered all through my body. The fishermen wore the kind of faces that belonged on the tins of shag tobacco; weather-beaten, wind-scoured, often sporting whiskers on which, when they bent down to offer toffee to me (it was sugar sugar sugar on

MOUSEHOLE
© Toby Millburn Pinn

the Estuary) I could still smell the brine. I wondered about those boats and pestered the men, without luck, to let me sail. They seemed little and tub-like and much too frail to brave the North Sea; but the nets and the peeled-away timbers were a vision of romance for me and they still are.

Many many years later on Cape Cod I sat with a glass of beer overlooking the Sound; a place mostly inhabited by summer visitors, most of whom belong somewhere in the Corporate World. And then someone came along with a plate of small, sweet shrimp, and beyond them I could see just the mast of a small fishing smack and all at once I was back in grey-green Leigh, with the slap of the water and the waves sucking at the shingle, and I was, for a moment, not in exile at all.

Born in London in 1945, Simon Schama is internationally acclaimed for his best-selling books which include: *A History of Britain, Volumes I-III* (2000-02); *Patriots and Liberators* (1977); *Citizens* (1989); *Landscape and Memory* (1995); and *Rembrandt's Eyes* (1999). His recent television series *A History of Britain* won several awards and was voted best history documentary by the readers of the *Radio Times*. He is currently Professor of Art History and History at Columbia University in New York.

LIFE BOAT STATION AT NIGHT
© Antony Messenger

BRIGHTON: FISHERMEN
© Chris Mole

BEACHY HEAD
© Chris Mole

River Cottage
Hugh Fearnley-Whittingstall

Although several valleys and ridges away from any possibility of a sea view, River Cottage is only about five miles, as the gull flies, from the sea. This sometimes seems odd to me, as when I am pottering in the garden, I tend to feel that I am entrenched deep in an inland rural Arcadia, so all-consuming that there is barely time, or mental space, to make room for the idea of a spectacular lime-cliffed coastline, dropping vertiginously to the gently contoured shingle beaches below – not to mention a vast expanse of sea beyond. So when, on some sunny summer evening, the pigs are fed and the day's work is done, the thought of a trip down to the coast sometimes strikes like a bolt from the green. The drive from River Cottage to the coast does not make the mental transition any more gradual. As the shoreline gets closer, the landscape doesn't dish out much in the way of clues. The rolling hills and gullies and the lush, loamy verges continue until I'm almost there. Winding my way through the pretty village of Eype on the way to my favourite beach, only the quaint house names – Sea Glimpse, or Shingle Tops – hint at what is imminent. Then comes the unmistakable taste of salt air. And as I sometimes forget around which bend it is that the sea can first be seen, I tend to brace myself. The final revelation still comes like a wave of light and noise that tingles the hair roots, just as it did when I arrived here as a child on holiday – after a drive of some four hours, not fifteen minutes. I like it like that. And though I would prefer to spend a lot more time on the coast and on the sea, especially now that I have a family, it still seems an unfeasible treat that it is there at all. When I do make it to the shore, I can revel in the rhythm of the waves, sipping at the shingle, then lift my eyes to the horizon and marvel at the sheer size and power of the water. It keeps me transfixed for, oh, minutes. And then I start to think about supper. Now that I have a small boat for potting and fishing, I try and make more time to get out to sea. Returning home with a few mackerel, a spider crab or even a couple of cuttlefish, to combine in the kitchen with some fresh vegetables from the garden, is the best possible way to forge a link between land and sea. And returning home empty-handed, as I not infrequently do, is not so bad either. At the very least I bring back a raging hunger. These days, a trip out on the boat to pull the pots is usually a family affair. The catching, cooking and eating of the fish is a blithe family communion, the profound joy of which is hard to express. But for me, part of the thrill is that Oscar seems, unprompted, to be making that vital, respectful connection, between life, death and the kitchen. It's a spark of understanding that fishing nurtures perhaps more than any other way of acquiring food.

Hugh Fearnley-Whittingstall's *River Cottage Cookbook* won the best food book award. Keen on cookery since he was a small child, he didn't train professionally, but instead studied at Oxford and travelled to Africa doing conservation work. Back in England, he became a *sous-chef* at the River Café, though he had to leave as he was too messy! Hugh has since become a familiar face on television with his series *Cook on the Wild Side* and *TV Dinners*. In 1997 he found River Cottage in Dorset, which led to two series being filmed there, *Escape* and *Return to River Cottage*. He is a keen supporter of the organic movement.

CORNWALL
© Joanna Eede

DUNGENESS
© Sophie Lindsay

TAKE-OFF
© Adam Davis

PUFFIN ON CLIFF
© Andy Thompson

COASTAL BALES
© Angela Maynard

LOW TIDE
© Angela Maynard

LOBSTER POTS
© Rupert Sagar-Musgrave

LIFEGUARDS
© John Coates

DECKCHAIRS
© John Coates

GRAND TOUR
© Angela Maynard

GATEWAY TO THE MOORS
© Joe Cornish

Thoughts...
Edward Fox

Excepting religious faith, an awareness of the extraordinary potential for goodness in humans and of the beauty of birds and animals…. how else can we know what God is, or might be? And how can Man be truly alive if robbed or debarred from an enduring contact with Nature – be it a hedgerow that borders an allotment patch, or the windy mountain crag?

I believe that Man is no more than the temporary steward of Nature, and must preserve her with devotion not just for his own, but for succeeding generations. The sight of neglected land by railway tracks, lazy hedgerow bashing by mechanical cutters and ugly storage buildings on farmland, devoid of sensitivity in their construction, are just three examples among countless other neglects of stewardship.

How fortunate that for every one of life's circumstances, Shakespeare, in beautiful expressive verse, encapsulates one's thoughts. I quote Duke Senior's speech from *As You Like It;* the last four lines are, in my view, piercingly succinct and relevant to today's world.

"Now, my co-mates and brothers in exile,
Hath not old custom made this life more sweet
Then that of painted pomp? Are not these woods
More free from peril than the envious Court?
Here feel we but the penalty of Adam,
The seasons' difference; as the icy fang
And churlish chiding of the winter's wind,
Which, when it bites and blows upon my body,
Even till I shrink with cold, I smile and say
This is no flattery; these are counsellors
That feelingly persuade me what I am.
Sweet are the uses of adversity;
Which, like the toad, ugly and venomous,
Wears yet a precious jewel in his head:
And this our life, exempt from public haunt,
Finds tongues in trees, books in the running brooks,
Sermons in stones, and Good in everything:
I would not change it".

Edward Fox has spent his career in the theatre, and has acted in numerous films, including *The Day of The Jackal* (1973), *The Go Between* (1971), *A Bridge Too Far* (1977), *Ghandi* (1982) and *Never Say Never Again* (1983). He loves and supports all aspects of rural Britain.

MOVING ON
© Jamie Campbell

The Valley
Rachel Johnson

My father, whose father first fell in love with this place, simply calls it, with a faraway look in his eye, 'The Valley.' Our family has been here since 1951. Not long compared to other local families, I know, but long enough for us to feel part of the Exmoor landscape.

There are three houses in the valley. The western-most house is a 15th-century longhouse, where my father and stepmother live. The middle house is my family's farmhouse to which we escape whenever London day-schools permit. The third and easternmost house in the straggling row is Aunt Birdie's cottage, a perfect Arts and Crafts fairytale dwelling, complete with rambling roses and peaked porch, its five windows casting an unblinking dark gaze across the Splat meadow, skipping over the Exe, to the steeply rising, bracken-clad hill beyond which lies the moor.

Aunt Birdie is the only one of us to live here all year round, and is very much custodian of the valley.

How did we get here? Luckily I have an invaluable resource to draw on – an unpublished memoir of my grandmother's called *Alas Poor Johnny*.

The author, born Irene Yvonne Williams in 1907, was half French. On the French side she was the descendant of troubadours from Alsace. She says Johnny, my grandfather, was the only presentable man she met whom she did not contemplate marrying. So, of course, she did. My grandfather hated the City, was awarded the DFC in the war, had four children and moved to Surrey, where they kept pigs and poultry.

'We heard of a hill sheep farm in the West Country which might suit us,' Granny writes, 'and Johnny rode down

CUMBRIAN VALLEY
© David Stephenson

FASCINATION
© Anthony Fisher

on his motorbike to see it. That night he got chatting to some of the locals in the bar of the White Horse at Bampton. One of them had been rabbiting a few days earlier at a farm near Winsford, and heard it was for sale. The place was so remote and inaccessible he couldn't imagine anyone ever wanting to live there.' The lads encouraged my grandfather to go and see it.

'The next night Johnny was back in the White Horse, buying them a drink in thanks. He'd liked the place so much he and the farmer had come to a verbal agreement on the spot.'

The farm is a sheltered oasis in the rugged isolation of the moor. Because of the height, the top farm is 1,300 feet above sea level, and the soil is unforgiving. It was nine years before my grandfather had his first holiday. Now, my father lets out the land to two local farmers and we mainly come here not to work, but to drink deep of the damp south west. Just as the family who lived here a century before us were the last on Exmoor to wear buckled shoes, our family has

staunchly resisted introducing mod cons, because we want the tone and atmosphere of the valley to remain.

Of course, my grandfather put in a bathroom instead of the Elsan, and my father has introduced two more 'new loos' into his longhouse. But the farm track remains as bumpy as ever. When my husband and I bought the farmhouse from my father, two years ago, we decided that we would do nothing to it at all.

As much as I love people discovering it for themselves, I love the fact that it is hidden and private. This is a bit of English paradise that will elude all but the most devoted hunters, walkers and riders and continue to pleasure, by its unchanging existence in the darkest countryside, my lucky family in particular for many years to come.

Rachel Johnson is a columnist on The Daily Telegraph. She is married to the lobbyist Ivo Dawnay, has three children and tries to spend as much time as possible on Exmoor, away from Notting Hill.

Ley Lines

Richard Madden

For me, the summer of 1992 was a strange and magical time. Living rough for a month in the fields and hedgerows of southern England may not be everybody's idea of fun. But a few physical discomforts were a small price to pay for the knowledge that I was following a sacred path that had not been trodden since Neolithic times.

I had been inspired by the work of two 'earth mysteries' specialists, Hamish Miller and Paul Broadhurst, whose now classic book *The Sun and the Serpent* proposed the tantalising proposition that there existed an ancient pathway of subtle energies connecting some of the most powerful ancient sites in Britain along an alignment running from just south of Land's End in Cornwall to the coast of East Anglia.

New-Age nonsense many would scoff – and did. But for my part, I was not in the least concerned. The truth or otherwise of Miller and Broadhurst's proposal did not change the fact that I would be walking through some of the most compelling landscapes in the country and visiting sacred spaces, wells, stone circles, temples, churches and burial mounds whose existence in the material world, at least, could not be disputed.

A Cornish childhood had given me a strong affinity with the many hundreds of ancient sites that punctuate the modern map of the British Isles. Most compelling were the stone circles that have stood for thousands of years on remote moorland locations, many pre-dating the construction

MOUNTAINS OF MOURNE
© David Kirk

KING ARTHUR'S HALL
© Paul Turner

From the start, my most profound impression was of seeing a familiar landscape with new eyes. Remote and lesser-known stone circles I had known since childhood were no longer stand-alone oddities but a series of sacred marker points, aligned according to the passage of the sun and moon at key times of the year. These 'chakra points' on the serpent body of the earth spirit had been sanctified by stone circles, dolmens and standing stones to ensure the healthy and fructifying flow of energy in some sort of sacred acupuncture, the secrets of which have long been lost.

However fanciful it might seem, I was aware of walking in a living landscape peopled by ancient god-like faces which stared down at me out of craggy rocks like incarnations of Blake's 'Ancient of Days'. One of the most striking was a monolithic pile of rocks on the western side of St. Michael's Mount looking out over the bay along the axis of the Serpent Line towards Land's End. Candles and votive offerings among the crags and lichen on the rock face confirmed that folk memories of these old beliefs still linger into modern times.

Along the way I would sometimes emerge from tranquil woodland to find myself in the suburbs of a town, the chaotic energies of the modern world swamping the subtle energies of the earth spirit. But always, as the cars, noise and light of the towns receded, the ancient energies would re-assert themselves once more.

One evening, alone in the middle of Dartmoor, I bivvied down overlooking a stream which wound its way along the floor of a shallow valley. I soon became convinced, due to a juxtaposition of subtle features in the landscape, that I was in the presence of a sacred site which had not been appreciated as such for thousands of years. It seemed to me at that moment as if I was in the presence of an ancestral intelligence working with the living spirit of the earth that had left a message encoded in the landscape. It lies there still; should we but choose to see.

of the pyramids. Silhouetted like jagged teeth against the night sky, these silent witnesses to the passing of pre-history into the space age often made me feel as if I had stumbled into a group of ancient, petrified wizards.

My walk took me through some of the oldest and most sacred sites in southern England: St. Michael's Mount near Penzance, the Hurlers and the Cheesewring on Bodmin Moor, St. Michael's Brentor on Dartmoor, Glastonbury Tor, Avebury and the Wittenham Clumps in Oxfordshire among many others. The regular appearance of place names, shrines or churches dedicated to St. Michael was no coincidence. The pre-Christian religions recognised the living spirit of the earth in the form of a dragon or serpent and the serpent-slaying Christian archangel denoted the subjugation of these old beliefs.

The idea of an ancient and long-hidden Serpent Line which coiled its way through the English countryside fascinated me. The authors had themselves dowsed the intertwining paths of the male and female aspects of the line during sorties over a period of many months. My plan was to follow the line with my own dowsing rods, but more in the spirit of a pilgrimage and a modern-day act of homage to ancient beliefs than in an effort to prove Miller and Broadhurst right or wrong.

Living rough seemed the right, if unconventional, option for two reasons. Firstly, I mourned the passing of the itinerant folk – a different breed to the urban homeless of today – who haunted the highways and byways of Cornwall in my youth. Secondly, I relished the idea of spending the night under the moon and stars in such spiritually charged spaces.

Richard Madden is a freelance travel writer and the adventure travel editor of *The Daily Telegraph*. He has also presented adventure travel documentaries for the Discovery Channel and is currently co-writing *The Daily Telegraph Book of Adventure Travel*.

The Night Sky
Libby Purves

The sky is our heritage too. When Oscar Wilde said 'We are all in the gutter but some of us are looking at the stars', it was still possible for that to happen. He died in 1900, in an age of gaslamps. He was never blinded to the night sky by neon and sodium, headlamps and electric hoardings and garish reindeer and Santas. The cities did not glow angrily up at the heavens in winter 1900, or even in 1950: they twinkled faintly. Even at the heart of those cities, a late-night reveller sodden with drink and sin might glance up and glimpse eternity. Another late Victorian writer, George MacDonald, wrote of a vagrant child looking up from the London streets on a cold night and seeing the moon... 'here was a cloud, all crapey and fluffy, trying to drown the beautiful creature. But the moon was so round, just like a whole plate, that the cloud couldn't stick to her. She shook it off, and shone out clearer and brighter than ever.....she's the only thing worth looking at in our street at night.'

Now, the city-dweller can see the moon still: but the stars, pinpricks of cold majesty in the black velvet mantle of the night, are strangers . We are trying to kill the mystery of the night. Look at satellite pictures of Europe, and populous areas – most of Britain, especially the south-east – glare up at the sky, with motorways and street lighting throwing as much light upwards as downwards. One of the most powerful arguments for National Parks is the fact that on the UK map you can see the boundaries of some of them – notably the Peak District – absolutely clearly, in detail, as black holes in the sea of glare. For what the satellite sees as blackness is, on earth, a rare boon: somewhere the stars can be seen from. Yet even in comparatively open country it is blanked out by road lighting, insensitive suburban lights in villages, and horrible (and fairly useless) security lights on private houses.

It must stop. The technology is available to make necessary lights throw less glare upwards; it should be promoted vigorously. There is a hunger for stars, still: a few years ago comet Hale-Bopp drew the nation out into open spaces to adore its long shining peacock tail, and the Perseid showers are reported on the news even though few of us can see them. Even the occasional satellite, bleeping across the sky, is a reminder of how small the greatest human achievement is, next to Nature's. We must cherish the night sky. As one Campaign for Dark Skies spokesman once said, 'the light from the rest of the Universe takes hundreds, thousands or millions of year to reach our eyes. What a pity to lose it on the last millisecond of its journey...'

Libby Purves is a writer and radio broadcaster. She has published eight novels and numerous non-fiction books, and is a main columnist for *The Times*. For 10 years she lived on a small organic horse-drawn farm in Suffolk with her husband, the writer Paul Heiney. The family still live in Suffolk, and are fortunate to be on a heath where the only interference with the night sky comes from Sizewell B nuclear power station three miles away.

STANDING STONES
© David Stephenson

STONE CIRCLES

There are more than 900 stone circles in Britain, although many have been badly damaged over the years. The oldest are thought to date from around 3000 BC and construction continued throughout the Neolithic period over the next 2,000 years. Some, like the great sites of Stonehenge and Avebury, are dramatic for their sheer scale and the organisation that must have been required to build them. It is hard to imagine they did not have a significant religious or ceremonial purpose , and there is evidence to support an astronomical function, but Britain's stone circles remain one of the most intriguing mysteries of the past.

Crop Circles as Land Art
John Haddington

Whatever views you may hold concerning the origins of the intriguing geometric shapes that appear each summer in the fields of England, you have to credit their creators with great artistic flair. Crop circles have been appearing since the mid-1970s, and have given rise to a completely new form of artistic endeavour. The first circles were small and hardly noticeable to the passing traveller. They were only some ten feet in diameter, so you would have to virtually trip over them to see them at all. Today the formations that are appearing with great regularity in the West Country and elsewhere are huge and complex mazes, the symmetry of which you can only make sense of from the air. Perhaps the most famous recent formation was the Chilbolton 'Face' of 2001. From the ground no discernible pattern could be seen, the flattened stems of wheat were swirled in a chaotic fashion round blocks of standing crop. But when you were airborne you could clearly make out the image of a man's face. Likewise, the huge array of 409 circles on top of Milk Hill, in the Vale of Pewsey, that appeared in August 2001, were placed so that from the ground the observer had no idea of the size of the formation. Only a small portion of it could be seen from any one position, due to the slope of the hill. This formation had a diameter of some 782 feet, and viewed from the air was perfectly symmetrical and quite magnificent.

I spoke to the farmer on whose ground the Milk Hill formation had appeared. He said that in previous years when he had been visited by other formations, he had been extremely sceptical, and viewed them as the creations of vandals intent on publicity making money out of photographs and fooling the gullible. He thought that it really was a diabolical liberty to use his land without his permission in this way. There is no doubt that a great many of the formations which appear each year are man-made, either with or without the permission of the farmers. However, he said that when he saw what had been made in his field that summer's night in August 2001, he was awestruck, and had had to admit to himself that it was beyond his ken.

Many of the more obviously man-made formations are great works of art. They take small teams of dedicated

CHILBOLTON FACE
© John Haddington

MILK HILL
© John Haddington

folk many hours to produce, under cover of darkness. The designs are dreamt up by artists and computer buffs, and the measurements are then transferred to the fields using a variety of methods, from high tech, to plank, garden roller and string. The results vary in quality, depending on the skill and sobriety of the teams involved, but most circle-makers are very careful to leave no trace of themselves in the completed work. Reports of a new formation and its position are soon received by researchers, and over-flights by photographers quickly organised to capture the image before it is trampled and damaged by visitors.

The custom now is that a farmer with a crop circle in his field, leaves an 'honesty box' at the entrance to his field, so visitors may donate a fee of £1 either to compensate him for the loss of crop, to raise funds for his parish church, or for other charitable causes. Others are unwilling to allow entrance to their fields at all.

At the end of the day everyone benefits in some way from these wonders in our summer fields, be they, artists, farmers, photographers, pilots of light aircraft and helicopters, B&B owners, or those that believe, like me, that some mysterious force is at work.

To learn more about this exciting phenomenon visit: http://www.cropcircleconnector.com

Lord Haddington is the 13th Earl of Haddington and lives in the Scottish Borders with his wife Jane and their three children. He farms 1,000 acres on his Mellerstain estate, raising beef cattle and growing cereals. He is an accomplished photographer and has founded 'Save our Songbirds' an independent charity which promotes the protection of songbirds through environmental improvements and the control of avian predators and domestic cats.

BLUEBELL RAILWAY
© Chris Mole

AMPHIBIOUS
www.mitsubishi-cars.co.uk © Golly Slater

TEAM WORK
© Robert Arthur

MAN, HORSE AND DOG
© Pauline Rook

SETTING OUT HER STALL
© Joanna Eede

Gypsy Horse Fair in Stow-on-the-Wold

Joanna Eede

Under a beech tree, in May sunshine, a gypsy called Eward is teaching me some basic Romany words. He stares at my face intently. 'Those are your *yacks*, and that is your *nacka*', he says, pointing to my eyes and nose. He cannot spell, so I transcribe phonetically. 'And those are your *vasters*, and those your *chocas*' – my hands and feet. 'But we're losing the language' he continues, '.... and it's important for our children to learn it so they can travel to Europe and talk to other gypsies.'

Hundreds of years ago legend has it that a talking white kitten led gypsies out of the woods and showed them the way to Stow-on-the-Wold, the highest of all Cotswold market towns, which defended itself against the Romans, and staged the last battle of the Civil War. The town was given the right in 1476 by King Edward IV to hold two gypsy fairs every year, in May and October. Romany gypsies from all over Britain still gather in a field on the road to Chipping Norton for one of Britain's 12 gypsy Fairs, where they trade their most precious commodity – horses.

I lap the town square twice before I can find an open café. Shops are boarded up and pubs are dark and empty as locals are wary of looting and violence. Over the years, the town council has repeatedly tried to close the 600 year-old event. 'It's ridiculous', says Vera Norwood, once a Tiller girl with Betty Boothroyd and now an honorary member of the Gypsy Council for her devotion to the Romany people, 'These are people who've bought big houses in the area and want their lives to be like a page out of *Homes and Gardens*, with no human diversity. There's little crime here with the gypsies'. A local journalist confirms that the police have not yet recorded a surge in crime coinciding with the gypsies' arrival in town, although they admit that two years ago several chickens went missing, only to be found in a suspiciously bedraggled state a few days later.

It's early, but the sloping field is packed with burger vans and trinket stalls; with women selling peach-coloured satin cushions and hand-painted milk churns. A man with a pencil-thin moustache, coloured neckerchief and tweed jacket shows me his box of squeaking lurcher puppies. I ask him about life on the road, 'We're the people of the highways and byways: the last people to be called in by God', he says, while his brother sells greasy black iron saucepans. Josie Lee, President of the Gypsy Council from East Ham in London, adds 'I see all my friends, catch up with all the news and buy things you can't buy anywhere else: gypsy china, coloured glass and hand-made wooden flowers. Otherwise we'd all have to go to Prague.'

Dave Rawlins has lived in his painted wagon all his life, and brought his children up on the road, mainly in Devon and Dorset. He sits on the front of his traditional caravan – called a Romany Vardo – and obliges a photographer by picking up his mandolin. Next door, a girl covered with gold jewellery is selling cut-price videos.

The atmosphere is friendly and, familiar. Men slap hands furiously as they broker a horse-deal. Cries of 'Whoa! Mind your backs!' send people swivelling to the corners of the field as trotting cart races take centre stage. A young boy rides bareback on a stocky piebald horse with traditional 'feathered' feet while a group of sassy teenage girls with bare midriffs peer at caged budgerigars.

However, the fair is forever under threat, as is much of gypsy culture throughout the UK. The ancient Horsmonden fair in Kent was banned in 2000 and a court injunction taken out in Stow threatens those who camp in

FIRST PRIZE, FROME SHOW
© Rose Hubbard

the field, although, given the Royal Charter, it will take an Act of Parliament to actually ban it entirely. As Vera Norwood says 'They gypsies own the field. They should be allowed to continue unimpeded. So many people in this country don't understand a way of life that is slightly different. We don't all live in square houses that never move. Travelling is the gypsies' culture, and they should be able to live freely'.

Joanna Eede was head of publicity for the Countryside Alliance Liberty & Livelihood March which took place on September 22nd 2002.

NANCY WALKER, VEGETABLE SELLER
© Pauline Rook

WORLD BOG SNORKELLING I
© Jon Crane

WORLD BOG SNORKELLING II
© Jon Crane

FIRST LIGHT, BARBURY CASTLE, WILTSHIRE
© Adam Dale

The Land of Liberty

Andrew Roberts

It is an ancient and fundamental principle of our liberty that a Briton can dispose of his justly-acquired property in whatsoever way he so desires. Indeed it is a principle far older than Britain itself, since it was an acknowledged right of free born Englishmen ever since the end of feudalism in the 14th century. So long as other Britons are not practically and measurably worse off, a Briton should be allowed to do anything he likes on, and with, that which is lawfully his. To upset that principle is to strike at the very heart of our constitution, our law, our customs, our history and our way of life.

To be allowed to hunt foxes across privately-owned land is thus a basic right that should not be curtailed by those who are in no way practically or measurably worse off because it takes place.

Hunting is undertaken because the property-owner wishes to cull his land of a pest in a manner that is traditional, enjoyable and exciting. Its so-called 'cruelty' is as

PLAITING
© Nina Wright

BELVOIR HUNT, HUNTSMAN, STAFF AND HOUNDS.
19TH JUNE 2001
© Gerry Wright

immaterial as it is unprovable, and is in no way analogous to bear-baiting and cock-fighting of earlier ages. When the anti-hunting lobby attempts to argue that fox-hunting is simply the modern equivalent of bear-baiting and cock-fighting they are simply wrong, for just as bears and cocks never posed a mortal threat to British poultry, so they also had no chance of escape in those cruel pastimes. (Were a bear or cock let loose in a hen coop they would not kill every single hen there, regardless of their own need for subsistence, as the fox does.)

Furthermore, for an animal like a fox to have rights, it would need to be shown that they also accept responsibilities towards other animals, for rights and responsibilities – as all philosophers from Socrates to Scruton have pointed out – must go hand in hand. Since the idea of a fox appreciating any responsibilities is a demonstrable absurdity, the anti-hunting lobby's arguments fall.

Only those for whom the rights of property hold no sway can believe that it is acceptable to dictate to a landowner what should or should not be done on his justly-acquired property. The present age has seen more imprecations upon the rights of property than any other since the Civil War, often in the spurious names of planning, compulsory purchase, health and safety, 'heritage', ramblers'

BROCKLESBY FOX HOUND
© Lee Beel
Bred by Lord Yarborough of the Pelham family since 1603, these heavy set Old English Hounds are never crossed within four generations of each other. The two packs – bitches and dogs – are known to comprise the best stock in the country. New blood is assiduously drawn from the purest breeds across Ireland and Wales tracing their ancestry back over hundreds of years.
Woe betide anyone who attempts to domesticate one of their puppies!

HATFIELD HUNT
© Richard Willock

MASSED HOUNDS OF THE SOUTH OF ENGLAND HUNTS
© Martyn Potter

access, and so on. To add the pained sensibilities of 'animal welfare' to that unedifying list would be a disgrace. Freedom is indivisible, and under threat.

Andrew Roberts took a first class honours degree in modern history at Gonville & Caius College, Cambridge, where he is an honorary senior scholar. Roberts' four-part BBC2 history series in 2003 coincided with his book *Hitler and Churchill: Secrets of Leadership*. He has two children and lives in Knightsbridge, London.

HANDSOME HOUND
© Tracey Jefford

THREE HOUNDS
© James Shepherd

HRH PRINCE OF WALES
© Martin Elliot

NOSES IN THE AIR
© Victoria Hunt

Hunting
Roger Scruton

I began hunting in my early forties. It was quite by chance that I should be trotting down a Cotswold lane on a friend's old pony when the uniformed centaurs came galloping past. One minute I was lost in solitary thoughts, the next I was in a world transfigured by collective energy. Imagine opening your front door one morning to put out the milk bottles, and finding yourself in a vast cathedral in ancient Byzantium, the voices of the choir resounding in the dome above you and the congregation gorgeous in their holiday robes. My experience was comparable. The energy that swept me away was neither human nor canine nor equine, but a peculiar synthesis of the three: a tribute to centuries of mutual dependence, revived for this moment in ritual form. This energy swept me away from my old life as a professor in London, to be washed up on a farm in rural Wiltshire, married to a pre-modern woman as deeply attached to hunting by upbringing as I had become by conversion.

Maintaining a small farm in modern conditions requires continual labour, and a resourceful imagination. Nothing pays for itself, and everything must be subsidised from some other source. Every now and then we ask ourselves whether it is worth it. And on hunting days we know that the question is absurd.

It begins on the day before, with a visit from the master, who goes from farm to farm securing territory. Ours is Wednesday country, and the master is a farmer, born and bred here. He has known the residents for three generations, and speaks in his broad Wiltshire accent with intimate understanding of the fields and coverts, as though he himself had charge of them. He tells you where he wants to go and his voice quavers with emotion, as though describing a favourite child. His role is like that of a priest, mystically transforming the landscape into a more spiritual version of itself.

VICTORIA HARRIS, TIVERTON HOUNDS
© John Burles

COTSWOLD HUNT
© Ann Chaffers

PICKING UP THE SCENT
© D. K. Martin

This mystical process is even more apparent on the day. You too are part of it, taken up by its ceremonial costumes, its ritual gestures and its quasi-liturgical words. We are up early, opening gates, dismantling wire, catching ponies and checking that the cows are secure. We set up a table with port, whisky and home-made cakes. And at half-past ten the followers begin to arrive. They come in battered cars, on bicycles, on horseback. Every trade is represented, from roofer to solicitor and from groom to vet. The distinction between the mounted followers and the rest is not one of class or wealth: the local plumber comes on horseback; the local landowner stumbles from field to field in her boots.

First to arrive is the band of retired farm-hands, led by Percy, who seems to have only two teeth – one upper and one lower – and who carries in his arms a one-eyed terrier with the same ratty grin as its master. They line the yard with earthy talk, greeting each new arrival with

BOXING DAY MEET AT HAGLEY HALL, WORCESTERSHIRE
© Victoria Hunt

HILLTOP CHASE
© Michael Sharp

enquiries about his sheep, his wife or his tractor, secure in the knowledge that their attitude to all these things is unquestionable and shared.

Some of the women wear tough country clothes, with wellies under woollen skirts. The younger ones have children in tow, and Rosalind leads her three-year-old daughter on a Shetland pony. The yard rapidly fills with people, and the verges with cars. At twenty-to-eleven the hunt box arrives, bringing the huntsman, the whipper-in, the kennel groom, the horses and the hounds. It stands in the centre of the yard, mesmerising people and animals with the hidden life that whines and whickers inside. The horses are now pirouetting in their stables and kicking the doors; conversation is warm and general, and the huntsman, descending slowly from the horsebox in his brilliant uniform, walks like a monarch through the sea of greetings.

In our country you are expected to give breakfast to the huntsman. What we had not expected, when our farm was visited for the first time, was a retinue like Lear's knights — kennel hands, whippers-in, terrier-men, farmers, rat-catchers, masters, ex-masters, and old boys for whom there is no explanation except that they have been around too long to need one — all stamping across the threshold in search of whisky, sausages and tea. Conversation touches every relevant subject from heifers to hedges and from scenting to sets.

NEW YEAR'S DAY, NORTH CORNWALL HUNT
© Benjamin Stansall

DARTING FOX
© David Talman

After 20 minutes, when the house is swollen with their talk and no longer ours, they go out into the yard. The tailboard of the box comes down, the hounds rush out into the sea of legs, and the horses come stamping down the ramp like angry troopers. The resemblance between the hundred gathered faces is not so much a matter of culture or breeding, as of life and landscape. Their faces shine with the same attachment to the place and the life which they are here to celebrate. The master gives a speech of thanks, and it is as though our membership has at last been recognised – but only on the understanding that the farm is common property and we its temporary trustees.

INTO THE WOODS
© Jane Body

LEAPING HOUNDS
© James Shepherd

WORRIED SHEEP
© John Eveson

ON THE RUN
© Sam Clark

WET HOUNDS
© Alan Hanson

MAN VS HORSE
© William Mollett

There is a short toot on the horn, and the pack assembles around the huntsman's horse, moving like a fluttering skirt towards the hillside. The band of horses, bicycles, cars and people moves like an exultant caravan across its collective territory, enjoying as a common possession what tomorrow will once more be parcelled into lots. And at the end of the day, when the huntsman and his 20 knights come clattering and mud-encrusted into our living room, loud, anecdotal and elated, we yield immediately, since the house, like the landscape, is theirs. We are not farmers but hunter-gatherers, equal partners in a common settlement. We have been granted a glimpse of another world, a world that we share with the animals, who are dignified as antagonists, worshipped as totems and pursued as quarry. You may welcome this or you may deplore it; but that is what hunting means.

Roger Scruton is a writer and philosopher who moved to the country on discovering hunting 15 years ago. His book on this subject – *Roger Scruton on Hunting* (Yellow Jersey Press) – was first published in 1998.

BEAGLES COMING HOME
© John Eveson

BORDER COUNTIES MINK HUNT
© Gail Greenhouse

FRESHWATER BAY
© Liam Thom

WALKING OUT, ISLE OF WIGHT
© Kay Gardner

THIRSTY WORK
© Neil McLaurin

The Blackmore and Sparkford Vale Hunt

Ivan Massow

I hunt with the Blackmore and Sparkford Vale. The truth is, it scares me witless. The grand sweeping proportions of Hardy's finest vale country are deceptively treacherous. Rain-thickened clay, already trampled, adds a foot or more to any jump. The hedges – tall and untrimmed – render both the horse and rider ignorant as to whether the rider in front is a length ahead, or has fallen and is waiting to floor them.

This vale is where my physical and mental limits are put to the test. It never ceases to amaze me that each rider can remain calm as their animal pushes forward for take-off, despite the melèe of ditch-knelt steeds and fallen riders.

This isn't sport in the modern sense of the word. Like gay, the word's meaning has changed around it. Hunting is about meeting the quarry on its own terms and giving it 'a sporting chance'. Hunting, for most, is about fronting up to the reality that is nature: beautiful and harsh. It is about watching the wind blowing through a coppice; about reading a million years of evolution as a twitch in your horse's flank presses you to take note of the direction of its ears. It's the

PINK COATS
© Ginni Beard

LOOKING FOR HOUNDS © Trudy Clarke
South & West Hunt, Golden Valley, Wiltshire

riders' mutual exchange as you ignore the high pitch of a hound wrongly excited by deer, or the squeak of a novice hound, over-zealous and over-excited. Both horse and rider acknowledge their mutual failure when they discover that their gaze has been fixed when the hounds starts speaking. His nose has been dragged here by a scent that might already have run on for half a mile. We are not there as spectators – we are there as eyes.

Then, suddenly, you know it's happened. There is no real noise, no one signal bearing proof – just a combination of a hundred tiny clues. The quarry has broken cover. No one moves: all you can do is look to the master. The hunt hierarchy is not just a matter of safety in such a dangerous pursuit. It's about respect for the order of things.

For a moment we amble, fearing a false alarm. The voluptuous echo of a fox pursued through the trees becomes cold reality as it breaks cover and takes a straight line in the open. Then there's no escape. Any promises you have made to yourself about 'taking it easy' fly out of the window. You are caught up in an almost primeval compulsion – as is your horse. You don't think to check or

to stop – and with up to a hundred horses flanking you, it would be too dangerous to try.

I do understand why people who haven't tasted this particular communion would want to ban hunting – although I think their faith in shooting is informed by Hollywood rather than reality. Hunting must seem pompous and dated. But kill it and you kill a breed of people who are no better or worse than anyone else but, like geologists or astronomers, have access to a particular understanding. Their modest contribution is to help humans make sense of the natural order of things and of our relationship with the elements. We live in a world surrounded by suction-packed, intensively farmed and perfectly delivered produce that ostentatiously proclaims itself as a fruit of the earth and sells in the name of palatability. Hunters, terrier-men, fishermen and the like, keep us from the Orwellian deceit that is our microwave nation.

Ivan Massow is a keen foxhunter He was chairman of the ICA, chaired the Mind enquiry into social exclusion and is heavily involved in the Prince's Trust. He now has two businesses – one which provides insurance to the gay community – the other which builds internet communities for use by affinity groups or as company intranets.

A Drop of Water and Hope: Angling

Charles Jardine

I am not entirely sure when you become an angler. Many maintain that to be an angler, you have to be born an angler. I am not convinced. I think that angling lures the onlooker in.

I believe also, that water is our 'glue'. It is the fascination and the mystery that transports us, the curious onlooker, from the elements that we know, to an abyss that we can seldom fathom.

Of course it is also not necessarily about catching fish – the fundamental that gives it the title is seldom the reason for doing it: ask any angler. I think that fishing exists for us to shake hands with nature more intimately than other pursuits usually allow. It is the stuff of ethereal evenings and early mornings in wild company. It is also about reality. Anglers know the struggle for life and the ever-present quicksilver path to death – they know, too, how insects surmount phenomenal odds, changing appearance and colour, and

CASTING, RIVER AYR
© Alister G. Firth

EVENING ON THE THAMES
© Mike Blewett

WINTER FISHING
© Mike Blewett

transport themselves from one incredible world to another. They are fantastic time and space travellers. The angler knows this, as they know the call of the otter and red shank and the silky movement of fish in ponds and rivers. It's not just about securing a quarry.

Every angler I know is an optimist at heart. They might hide it well under a cloak of dejection and pessimism but there is always a conviction that next time will be better.

I cannot pass a pond, lake or river without having a quick, darting look. Utterly irrational. Why? Simply because we are anglers. I have passed over bridges in town centres and gazed at the aquatic travesty below: oily currents negotiating shopping trolleys and traffic cones, the consumer world's garbage spread like tatty wallpaper across a water world; yet I still hope to catch a glimpse of a darting piscine shape.

It is a madness of sorts, too. Why else would we shiver through frosts, fish for pike in blizzards, burn ourselves to a crisp in boats at the height of summer when every sensible trout is resting in over 40 feet of water in a state of torpor. Why do we venture out at bat flight and spend our time in wild company for a brief encounter with tench, bream or carp? Why, too, when fishing for sea trout, do we immerse ourselves in the darkest nights imaginable on rivers offering

FISHING IN SCOTLAND
© W. P. Andrews

FAMILY WATCHING, RIVER AYR
© Alister G. Firth

nothing more than odd sounds and a silvery fractured thread for guidance, our ears sensitive to every rustle and creek?

However, I do know when I became an angler; it was on a cold February day, over 40 years ago, on the Kentish Stour in Fordwhich. The river was as sullen as the landscape and the water coiled darkly around sienna reeds and umber weeds; the bright spark in the gloom was my float top — jaunty and red it sailed magnificently down the stream, the line tumbling after it in seductive spirals. Below, the maggots danced their jig of fishy allure. Periodically the float would stutter, hiccough, then twitch under: it was momentary, fleeting but oddly positive — a swift lift of the rod, then that

pulsating and electrifying piscine resistance. The fish my father and I caught were chrome-bright, crimson-finned roach that lit up the sepulchral backdrop. Their beauty transfixed me then, as it does now. I may have fished before that day, but it was only then I became an angler and knew the 'divine madness' of a true, life-long affliction. My son, too, has caught it. Being cursed by angling is many things: none I suggest, bad.

Charles Jardine fishes. He lives to fish. He writes about fish; paints, draws and photographs fish. He likes being in places where fish are. Jardine would also like it known that he will fight tooth-and-nail to protect the sport and the creatures and places that he feels so passionately about.

HIGH BIRD AT DUSK
© Steven Barker

Shooting
Max Hastings

For ten thousand years or so, it did not occur to man, the hunter, to justify the pursuit of quarry species, other than by bringing home food for the pot. But over the past few centuries, we have been gradually moving into a new era. Though fishers and shooters continue to eat what we kill – and it will be a bad day when we cease to do so – pleasure and personal fulfilment have become the chief purpose of sport. We are no longer hunter-gatherers in the traditional sense.

The changing nature of field sports means that those who practise them are asked to justify themselves, in a way that would have been unimaginable to our ancestors. My father used to assert with relish that 'death and sex are the principal business of our countryside'. Everyone familiar with the wild places knows that he was right.

Hunters of every kind are participating in a process of selection, cropping and predation which is a fundamental throughout the natural world. But a significant number of people today believe that it is wrong for mankind to take part in the culling process, and demeaning that human

WAITING GUN
© M.W. Bews

TOMMY AND HOUND PUP
© David Mason

HOME
© Ray Moffatt

hunters should gain pleasure from killing wild creatures.

One of the most important counter-arguments that hunters, shooters and fishers make is that we put into the environment far more than we take out of it. Almost everyone who pays money to take part in field sports is funding the cause of conservation, making a practical contribution to the welfare of the countryside of a kind that few advocates of 'animal rights' can match.

The Game Conservancy Trust has been conducting research to demonstrate this case for over half a century.

Since 1990, it has managed farmland at Loddington in Leicestershire on behalf of its Allerton Project. Everybody who is interested in field sports should be interested in Allerton. Its scientific findings are vitally important. Before the GCT took over, the land was unkeepered.

Over the past 13 years, thanks to a programme of habitat enhancement and vermin control, the wildlife population at Loddington has bloomed on a remarkable scale. The public at large will never care about populations of game species, especially those that are reared for shooting. But the

EJECTOR
© Jason Dawson

PENSIVE MAN AND HOUND
© Lucinda Marland

Allerton figures show that songbirds and hares prosper amazingly thanks to shooting management.

Today, the programme has entered a new phase. Keepering has been withdrawn from Loddington, so that researchers can show what happens to wildlife if the land is not stewarded for sport. Few countrymen will be surprised to know that early statistics already show a significant decline in songbirds. The Game Conservancy is conducting another project in Yorkshire, which similarly demonstrates the benefits to all kinds of wildlife.

Much of the public still believes that conservation means leaving the countryside to its own devices, 'in a state of nature'. This is, of course, a delusion. Wildlife prospers best where the landscape is carefully and expensively managed. Those who shoot and fish pay willingly from their own pockets to achieve this. If there was no sport, the taxpayer would have to pay huge bills to preserve from natural predators, the birds and animals it professes to love.

It is not enough merely to assert that field sports enhance the landscape and bring great benefits to wildlife of all kinds. We must continue to generate evidence to make the case. It is a pity that the public does not extend to the Atlantic salmon, for instance, the arbitrary and selective enthusiasm it lavishes upon seals, otters, foxes, even cormorants. Our responsibility is to keep patiently explaining

DAY'S PHEASANT SHOOTING
© Pete Gelly

COURSING
© David Mason

some of the realities of the countryside to anyone willing to listen. It is a difficult business. We should recognise that nobody will ever be impressed by arguments about the welfare of grouse, partridges, pheasants. But we do have a final story to tell about all manner of birds and beasts which the public values. They may not come to love hunters, but they can learn to recognise how much hunters contribute to the countryside, and for everything that dwells there.

Sir Max Hastings was educated at Charterhouse and University College Oxford. He was editor of *The Daily Telegraph* (1989-95), after which he became editor of the *Evening Standard* (1996-2002).

BEN'S PRIDE
© Ray Moffatt

SUNSET ON A NORFOLK BEACH
© Kay Gardner

FERRET FANCIER
© Deborah Husk

Ferreting

Johnny Scott

Ferrets and ferreting, fieldsports' poor relations, have moved up in the world and not before time. Ferreting's lineage is surely as ancient as hunting and hawking – nomadic Black Sea tribesmen were bolting sousliks and marmots with their steppe polecats hundreds of years before Christ, but it has always lacked the social cachet of hunting with hound or hawk.

Rabbits and the art of working a ferret were introduced by the Normans – the first pictorial record of a rabbit in British history is amongst the embroidery on the robes in which St Cuthbert's skeletal remains were wrapped for transportation from Lindisfarne to Durham Cathedral around 1100. Warreners who ran the great artificial rabbit warrens, never achieved the status of huntsmen or falconers and ferreting was always considered a working man's sport. Essentially a countryman's activity, ferreting has been, since the shift in population from country to town that started with the Industrial Revolution, one of the ways urban sportsmen maintained contact with their rural background and thousands of ferrets are kept in the backyards of Britain's housing estates.

Despite its lowly status, ferreting has long been recognised as the ideal way to introduce a child to fieldsports. Owning a ferret teaches them the responsibility and common sense that are essential in handling working animals, particularly ones that bite. After a little tuition, ferreting provides them with the opportunity to discover our vanishing countryside unsupervised and learn about wildlife from their own mistakes.

Best of all, when they get it right, a child experiences that wonderful sense of achievement in bringing something home for the pot. Nowadays, with the emphasis on educating the young about their priceless but threatened heritage, there is no shortage of people in the British

FERRETER
© Becky Griffiths

END OF THE DAY
© Slawko Berezynskyj

THE BAG
© Anthony Fisher

THE GARRON (OPPOSITE)
© David Mason

Association for Shooting and Conservation and the Countryside Alliance willing and eager to help them get started. There are over 140 game and country fairs up and down the country from April to October, each with its ferret stand and an expert on hand from one of the many ferret organisations, to give advice on welfare and the practicalities of ferreting.

Furthermore, there are an incredible number of ferrets kept simply as pets. I think there were two million of them at the last count. Like other pets, ferrets sometimes become victim to abuse and neglect or are simply abandoned when they cease to amuse. Over 50 rescue centres run by volunteers care for these casualties, funded in part by ferret shows and breed competitions. The highlight of these enormously popular events is ferret racing.

Competing ferrets, vociferously encouraged by their owners, gallop down 33-foot tubes over a series of eliminator heats. At least that is the theory. Some repay the months of training and last the course – others perversely turn round half way down the tube and rush back to the start line, or curl up and go to sleep. Occasionally, a ferret exceeds expectations – like that owned by an elderly lady from Belford in Northumberland, which covered the distance at the North of England Ferret Racing Championships recently, in a scorching 11.46 seconds. It saw off the other 200 competitors and rocketed to national prominence as the *Guinness Book of Record's* fastest ferret.

Sir Johnny Scott is a farmer, journalist, author, broadcaster and co-presenter of the television series *Clarissa and the Countryman*.

UNDER AN ENGLISH SKY
© Mary Turner

BOOTS ON GRASS
© Mary Turner

STAG CALLING
© Paul Turner

HORSE SHOWER
© Bill De La Hey

HORSE
© Chris Mole

THE MARCH, SEPTEMBER 2002
© Henny Goddard

The March

407,791 Came to be Counted

James Stanford

There were 407,791 marchers, a further 119,000 'marching in spirit', and 2,250 coaches from throughout the United Kingdom and Ireland. There were special trains from 35 starting points, representatives from at least 30 other countries and more than 1,000 rural organisations. They all invaded London on Sunday 22nd September 2002 under the overall direction of the Countryside Alliance.

From dawn, as the first flecks of autumn dimmed the plane trees in the Royal Parks, they began to congregate. Coaches from as far away as Forres on the Moray coast and the very tip of Cornwall nosed their way into Park Lane or Southwark Street and, with quiet good humour, the passengers joined the gathering crowds in Hyde Park or on the Embankment at Blackfriars. London awoke to never-ending convoys of coaches and ever-flowing streams of people disgorging from the mainline stations at Liverpool Street, King's Cross, Waterloo and Paddington.

Those who were there will never forget the politeness and the extraordinary discipline of that volunteer army. Despite the difference in backgrounds, interests and activities, they were absolutely united on one point: they all saw the proposed hunting legislation as the 'last straw' in their dealings with Government. No better name could have been coined for the march than 'Liberty and Livelihood': both were at stake.

PAINTED LADY
© Andrew Bruce

© Leila Adams

© Adrian Fisk

© Peter Glenser

© Peter Glenser

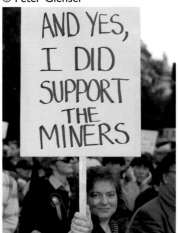

© Peter Glenser

© Peter Glenser

© Peter Glenser

© Peter Glenser

© Peter Glenser

© Peter Glenser

Six hundred years after Wat Tyler led the Peasants' Revolt, the countrymen and women of Britain and those who love its countryside, had declared that a line had to be drawn.

The marching crowds included princes, dukes, parliamentarians, former cabinet ministers and media celebrities. Even a pair of newly-weds fresh from their celebrations joined the march still in their wedding finery. Alongside them marched fishermen, jockeys, gamekeepers, coursing people, terrier-men, together with thousands of people who shoot and hunt including chasseurs from around the world, many of whom visit the UK every year and bring much-needed support to rural economies. Perhaps most noticeable of all was the vast numbers of children. From infants in their parents' arms to teenagers and university students, everyone seemed to sense that it

would be a hugely significant day in our rural history.

This would be the last peaceful march, and accurate number-counting was crucial. The final tally, confirmed by the Metropolitan Police after the most methodical count ever conducted at such an event, was nearer to 430,000. [The subsequent Peace Rally held in London prior to the 2nd Gulf war has been claimed by police – with no counting procedure in place – to be bigger, though in fact this was of a significantly shorter duration and over no greater distance.]

As Big Ben struck 10.00am, the two marches began to edge forward, slowing or speeding up at intervals to ensure that the carefully choreographed merger in Whitehall should go to plan. As precisely as guardsmen, the 'Liberty' march, after passing along Pall Mall and Trafalgar Square, streamed into Whitehall just as the 'Livelihood' marchers came into sight in Whitehall Place. Barely a yard separated them as they

© Peter Glenser

© Peter Glenser

© Peter Glenser

© Peter Glenser

© Peter Glenser

© Peter Glenser

© Peter Glenser

© Isobel Hutchison

© Peter Glenser

© Peter Glenser

© William Mollett

© Peter Glenser

© Isobel Hutchison

© Peter Glenser

© Peter Glenser

© Peter Glenser

MARCHING TO THE PIPES
© Adrian Fisk

joined and marched on side by side to the skirl of pipes, banners aloft, past the Cenotaph and Downing Street into the wide space of Parliament Square.

Few will forget the moment when they walked past the Cenotaph in silence, save for the lament of a single piper. Nor perhaps the final few yards as they passed the electronic counter and saw themselves silhouetted on the vast video screen mounted in front of Parliament.

It was a day for the record books, and perhaps a day that, despite their studied absence and their determination to deride its significance, even the politicians could not overlook. Those who live and work and have their being in 'England's green and pleasant land' rose up, often at great personal inconvenience and cost, to remind those who walk in the gilded corridors of Whitehall and Westminster, that unjust laws based on prejudice and ignorance will never be tolerated.

James Stanford was chairman of David Brown engineering group, he then became director general of Leonard Cheshire, the world's largest disability charity. He recruited and led the teams that organised the Liberty & Livelihood March in London in September 2002. He hunts in Dorset and shoots a few days each year.

PORTRAIT OF A FARMER
© Jo Hunt

LOBBYING IN PARLIAMENT SQUARE, 2003
© William Mollett

THE AFTERMATH
© Susannah Webb

ROAD KILL
© Peter Dazeley

The Future

Farming
Zac Goldsmith

The principal sculptors of our countryside are farmers, and as they are under unprecedented pressure, there's one thing we can all predict without fear of being wrong – that the British countryside is going to change dramatically over the coming years.

The question is how? If current trends continue – if the agricultural establishment, namely the Government, National Farmers' Union and the giant food conglomerates – has its way, then the changes will be invariably for the worse. That is my opinion, of course, but poll after poll has demonstrated that it is also the opinion of the vast majority of people, farmers and consumers.

And there's a very good reason for this. The establishment has set itself the task not of finding solutions to the rural crisis, but of managing it. Time and again, the message from government and big producers is that a further erosion of our farm base is not only inevitable but necessary. If the market is allowed to select naturally the global economy's most efficient players, so the argument goes, then Britain's backward farmers will benefit from long-overdue streamlining.

Within the narrow context of their peculiar worldview, they're right. Small farmers can't realistically compete with giant monocultures in the south – or not without endless subsidies. For some to have a chance of being internationally competitive, many others would have to go. But why should they? What good would subjecting Britain's farmers to the brutality of the global economy actually achieve? More importantly, what would be the consequences?

Small farms are already giving way to larger farms, and farm workers are already leaving the land, *en masse*. So it's not hard to imagine where trends will lead us. A handful of small 'museum' farms will remain, dominated by large expanses of industrial agriculture, for which land itself is little more than a coincidence. The physical countryside will

REDUNDANT FARM BUILDINGS, LINCOLNSHIRE
© Wanda Sooby

OLD JOE, AGED 87 © Marilyn Hardman
Struggling to continue farming.

MILKING PARLOUR
© Ian Geering

increasingly resemble the industrial wasteland that has enveloped much of the United States, where topsoil is being lost faster than it can be replenished, and where the only species that prosper are monocrops and the pests that eat them.

For consumers it means an increasingly distant agricultural system. Their only connection with the produce they eat will be the safety assurances of anonymous bureaucracies. For the environment, it means heightened dependence on fossil fuels – the prime cause of climate change – with basic foods being flown thousands of miles from field to plate.

Britain's reliance on an increasingly volatile global economy will be exaggerated still further. Come wind or high water, we will have to be able to access basic food from foreign lands for more than 60 million people on a daily basis. It means that the global trading system cannot falter, even for a while. And as we pave over the last of the greenbelt, as we replace priceless local knowledge and technical know-how acquired over generations, it's going to be harder and harder to turn back.

But thankfully, as we know, trends rarely continue indefinitely. People don't want nuclear-irradiated food shuttled in from the other side of the world. People don't want a ghost-town Britain. They don't want farmers to become plumbers or computer technicians, as Lord Haskins suggested, even if it

QUARANTINED BY FOOT-AND-MOUTH
© Ian Geering

TRADITIONAL HAYMAKING
© Brian Jordan

POPPIES
© Martin Elliot

would satisfy one abstract economic principal or another. They want – we all want – is a countryside where farmers are valued, where food production is directly supervised by consumers themselves, where animals are reared by human beings for human beings and not on conveyor belts for distant markets.

The agricultural experts pompously regard themselves as realists. But if they are, then reality doesn't add up. They bemoan the subsidies heaped upon farmers to keep them in business. But they fail to recognise that the benefits of those subsidies to ordinary farmers aren't a patch on the market distortions that are bankrupting them. They yearn for a free market. But what kind of 'freedom' involves heaping bogus regulations on small producers at the behest of the multinationals? What role does 'freedom' play in using taxes to cover the indirect costs of industrial farming? What is the point

LINSEED
© Martin Elliot

WALLACE BOUNDY, BACHELOR © WANDA SOOBY
Wallace continues to farm in the way his family have since the 1960s.

of providing free infrastructure so that the giant traders can access and out-compete every market on earth? How can we even use the term 'free market' when two organisations alone control 80% of the world's grain trade?

The tide of public opinion is flowing away from the madness of this false economy. Sooner or later our policy makers will catch on, either in response to that shift, or because natural conditions will force change. Human-scale, diverse agriculture not only answers the call of the environment, consumers and farmers themselves: it is the only true hedge we have against social and climatic instability, both of which the signs suggest will exacerbate. Change will happen. Let's hope it's on our terms.

Zac Goldsmith has been the director and editor of *The Ecologist Magazine* for six years. Prior to that he worked for a number of years with The International Society for Ecology and Culture, based in California (USA), Bristol (UK), and Ladakh (India) where he also ran a tourist education programme.

TRACTOR © Wanda Sooby
A tractor that Wallace Boundy uses. Characters like Wallace have little future due to the way modern farming works now.

Modern Rural Architecture
Lucinda Lambton

DESERTED FARMHOUSE, YORKSHIRE DALES
© Susan Leedale

INSIDE DESERTED FARMHOUSE, YORKSHIRE DALES
© Susan Leedale

Never a day goes by without my bashing my head against a brick-cladding wall, wailing at the progressive nationwide eroding of the vernacular; damning the pox that we are allowing to disfigure the face of Britain. From Banff to Bognor and from Newcastle to Newquay it is fast spreading, scarring our countryside, towns and cities with eruptions of grotesquely unsuitable houses, built in styles and materials that pay no courtesy whatsoever to their surroundings.

Swathes of scandalous cheap-jackery and jim-crackery of the neo-Tudor, neo-Georgian and the neo-vernacular – in fact neo-nothings – are infecting our land and our very lives. The sheer ubiquity of these buildings could brainwash the new generation into assuming they represent the acceptable face of British architecture with all sense of national as well as local culture annihilated by the corporate culture creating them.

Soon plastic 'period' doors will be standard, surrounded by plastic 'period' porches. Soon PVC garage doors will be accepted as the main architectural 'feature' of the house, along with windows of stick-on 'lead' paning. Worst of all are the PVC-u windows which are disfiguring façades both new and old – the very eyes of Britain's buildings being gouged out and replaced by those of dioxin-ridden plastic.

Who is responsible for these abominations nationwide; the planners or the developers, the landowners or the architects? Time and time again when one tries to pin them down, the finger is helplessly pointed elsewhere. Should the Government not set up a 'supremo' to guide them on a responsible way forward?

How can we stand by and allow this to happen? If buildings reflect the tastes, the dreams and the ideals of the age, what will these buildings reflect of our ideals today? If ever there was proof of mammon reigning supreme, then it is to be seen with these soulless, corporate coffer-filling excrescences which we are allowing to sprawl over the face of Britain.

There are of course happy exceptions. There are heroes countrywide, who are creating new buildings and restorations which dignify, rather than despoil, their

VILLAGE SURGERY
© Andrew Storm

surroundings. Charles Morris, whose innovative modern lines burst forth from the seemingly ancient bodies of his buildings, is one. Neil Holland is another, whose buildings seem to have grown out of the body of the land. 'People who live in a certain place on the earth become part of it' he says 'And they build accordingly and there is a kind of resonance.... a symphonic relationship'.

HRH The Prince of Wales was a huge influence on architectural excellence in British housing development when he conceived Poundbury, and commissioned its master plan from Leon Krier. Today this development, with John Simpson's beautiful Market Hall in lively use, has come of age and its influence worldwide has been enormous.

As for its influence in the West Country – go for yourselves and raise a glass to the splendidly substantial flint, stone and thatched pub at nearby Stratton. Standing proud on the village green, showing off local materials in all their splendour, and seeming for all the world to have been the centre of village life for hundreds of years, it was in fact built only months ago.

But I do not want merely to trumpet tradition, rather I mean to damn the developer's trumped up version of it duping the nation into accepting it as part and parcel of our land. This is not a rant for 'revivals', far from it. It is a plea for architectural integrity. Design with style; build properly with proper materials; when possible using what is local to the land, and whatever you design.

A good example is to be found on the banks of the Thames in Oxfordshire. Two buildings stand side by side; one in today's neo-Tudor by Barratt Homes, the other, by the architect John Outram, in a masterful mix of Egyptian and inventive lines, built in brilliantly-coloured concrete. While the so-called 'vernacular' sticks out like a suppurating sore thumb, the Egyptian House sits like an exotic jewel in the landscape.

Lucinda Lambton is a writer, photographer and broadcaster who works both behind and in front of the lens, nosing out architectural flights of fancy. She was elected Honorary Fellow of the Royal Institute of British Architects in 1997. Married to the journalist Peregrine Worsthorne, Lucinda has two sons by a previous marriage and lives in Buckinghamshire.

The Future of Farming and Food
The Right Reverend John Oliver, Bishop of Hereford

OLD JOE'S SHED
© Marilyn Hardman

It was a late summer evening in north Devon, and the Barnstaple branch train was ambling along the Taw Valley, through lush water-meadows, and past fields in which the wheat was standing in stooks – grown as much for thatching straw as for the grain. Red Devon cattle and sheep grazed beside the line, whilst ancient farmhouses and the sturdy stone towers of Devon churches were occasionally visible.

It was only 20 years ago, and yet it seems a very different age – in some ways an idyllic time for farming and rural life. Prices for most farm products were reasonably good, village life flourished, and local produce was on sale at the pannier markets in Barnstaple and South Molton. There were also jobs available in the newly-established chipboard factory, which processed local timber in a suitably sustainable way.

Of course there were other things happening elsewhere. In East Anglia intensive arable farming was having a deeply damaging effect on the environment and biodiversity (words which were then heard only on the lips of a few enthusiasts). The unsustainable Common Agricultural Policy was fuelling a farming boom that could not last; the farming industry was soon to enter a time of sharp decline, with globalisation, the power of the supermarkets and a strong pound causing economic havoc to its communities across Britain.

What of the future of farming and food production? It is possible to discern some trends, but the long-term picture is unclear. Funds *are* being switched from product subsidy towards agri-environment and rural-infrastructure schemes, but the sums are too small to bridge the gap between production costs and the depressed prices on offer.

There will be contradictory pressures: on the one hand temptations for the larger farmers to increase the scale and efficiency of production, in order to compete on world markets; while smaller farmers seek out niche markets for premium-priced products, concentrating on high-quality,

WENSLEYDALE

© Judges Postcards Ltd

organic or rare-breed production, or on ways to add value before the primary produce leaves the farm gate. Increasingly, farmers will look for other sources of income, from letting property, converting barns, catering for leisure pursuits, producing energy crops, or by combining care for their own land with contract work on somebody else's. Significant acreages are already owned by incomers, who buy a 50–100 acre farm, often with a real commitment to sustainable and environmental land management, but offering no guarantee of long-term stability of use.

The acceleration of climate change will lead to new patterns of cropping, and in terms of wildlife, will cause both the extinction of some species and the flourishing of others relatively new to temperate climes. But with global warming will come more extreme weather patterns – high winds, drought and flood, all more common than in the past, creating yet more hazards and yet more uncertainty for those who care for the land. And there will be continuing pressure on rural areas and on rural communities, as more and more people choose to escape from urban life into an increasingly crowded countryside.

One important and imponderable fact is public taste. If there were to be a significant increase in demand for home-produced food, a concern with food security, and a backlash against the current obsession with cheapness and convenience (not to mention the animal welfare implications or the conditions in which food is produced on the other side of the world), then farmers could really look forward to the future with confidence, and feel once more that they had a valued and trusted part to play in national life.

The Right Reverend John Oliver, Bishop of Hereford, was educated at Westminster School and Gonville and Caius College Cambridge. He was an assistant curate in Norfolk from 1964-68, the chaplain and assistant master at Eton College 1968-72 and a Devon vicar 1973-82. His hobbies include motorcycling, railways, music, and architecture.

WHAT WILL BECOME OF FARMING
An in-depth conversation over the farm gate between the photographer's father and his neighbour. © Katherine Owen

TOO TIRED TO WALK HOME
© Gail Greenhouse

THE EDITORS

William Mollett's plan to create a photographic book in celebration of the countryside by launching a competition in *The Daily Telegraph* was inspired by a conversation with his wife on the morning after the Countryside Alliance March. As a Lincolnshire farmer's son with a Polaroid camera at the age of nine, he has returned to his youth after a career in surveying. He is a founding director of Travelman Publishing, lives in London and has one son.

Joanna Eede's idea for *Liberty and Livelihood — a Portrait of Rural Britain* was born out of her work as head of publicity for the Countryside Alliance March of the same name on September 22nd 2002. It stemmed also from her belief that Britain is increasingly disconnected from nature, rural life and seasonal cycles. The book is a tribute to her grandmother, with whom, as a child, she spent long summers in Aberaeron, a remote town in West Wales.

Robin Page
Caroline Waldegrave
Kate Hoey
Henry Hobhouse
Philip Mould
Duff Hart-Davis
Nicholas Crane
Bishop of Bath & Wells
Sandy Gall
Julian Fellowes
Rachel Johnson
Richard Madden
John Haddington
Andrew Roberts
Charles Jardine
James Stanford
Lucinda Lambton
Bishop of Hereford

A celebration of the countryside as seen through the eyes of many of today's leading exponents and enthusiasts. Their contributions are accompanied by a wide array of arresting and unusual photographs selected from the nationwide photographic competition launched by *The Daily Telegraph*.

ISBN 1-86092-024-1

9 781860 920240